NORTH
STAR
WAY

NOW
OR NEVER

NOW
OR NEVER

Your Epic Life in 5 Steps

THE BRIDGE FROM WHERE YOU ARE TO WHERE YOU WANT TO BE

ALEXI PANOS
AND PRESTON SMILES

NORTH STAR WAY

NEW YORK   LONDON   TORONTO   SYDNEY   NEW DELHI

North Star Way
An Imprint of Simon & Schuster, Inc.
1230 Avenue of the Americas
New York, NY 10020

First North Star Way hardcover edition December 2016

NORTH STAR WAY and colophon are trademarks of Simon & Schuster, Inc.

For information about special discounts for bulk purchases, please contact Simon & Schuster Special Sales at 1-866-506-1949 or business@simonandschuster.com.

The North Star Way Speakers Bureau can bring authors to your live event. For more information or to book an event, contact the North Star Way Speakers Bureau at 1-212-698-8888 or visit our website at www.thenorthstarway.com.

Interior design by Jaime Putorti

Manufactured in the United States of America

10 9 8 7 6 5 4 3 2 1

Library of Congress Cataloging-in-Publication Data is available.

ISBN 978-1-5011-3160-8
ISBN 978-1-5011-3164-6 (ebook)

CONTENTS

Real isn't how you are made . . . It's a thing that happens to you.

It doesn't happen all at once. You become. It takes a long time. That's why it doesn't often happen to people who break easily, or have sharp edges, or who have to be carefully kept. Generally, by the time you are Real, most of your hair has been loved off, and your eyes drop out and you get loose in the joints and very shabby. But these things don't matter at all, because once you are Real you can't be ugly, except to people who don't understand.

—Margery Williams, *The Velveteen Rabbit*

NOW
OR NEVER

INTRODUCTION

Well, well, well, look who's here. Hello, you sexy beast! We couldn't be more excited to share this journey with you. Our excitement comes from knowing that, whether you know it or not, you've just committed to blowing past ordinary to embrace the extraordinary life that is yours to claim. You've picked up a book that's about leaving behind the mundane to step into the magical.

We've broken it down into five powerful steps.

1. You always have a choice.

2. Be radically responsible.

3. Act now.

4. Own who you are.

5. Have a blast.

The five steps are really quite simple, yet extraordinarily profound. If you master even ONE of these, we can almost guarantee that your experience of life will shift dramatically. Start putting all five into practice? Well, that combination just might set off a ripple effect of goodness throughout your entire universe that changes you forever.

We've come to understand that the answer to all of your problems is the same: YOU. Now, so often we say that we want our lives to be different; we yearn to have more and to be better. And you certainly deserve *all* of that. But the only person who can deliver this to you IS YOU. You are the sole author of your life, and instead of searching for your happiness in a new person, a new job, a new city, a new home, or new clothes, we've laid out the formula to create inner happiness from *within*. (Then anything external is a bonus—sweet!) And the beauty is, you have everything you need to create inner greatness *right now*. No matter what job you have, what partnership you're in or not in, how much you do or do not have in the bank—you can start from right where you are and create some magic with these five steps.

We're living in new times, with humans facing a set of challenges that no other generation has ever had to face. Technology has changed just about everything, and yet some things remain: our will to thrive and grow into the greatest versions of ourselves. Yet so many of us walk around like zombies staring into little minicomputers, oblivious to what's actually happening in and around us. We live in a time when it's quite literally NOW or never. Where we either choose to find a way or to fade away.

Most people have bought into the lie that *someday* is where it's at—that their dream life is somewhere off in the future—but your life is not out there in someday land. It's right here, and it's ready for the taking. We wrote this book for those of you serious about answering the call. We wrote it for those of you who are tired of bullshitting your life away and are ready to step it up in all areas . . . *powerfully*.

A little background on us. We've been traveling the globe leading workshops, speaking, writing books, and making videos like wild banshees because we love, love, love the human experience and feel it is our duty to leave as many people as possible with tools that will support them in living their best lives now. And by now, we mean NOW. Because we live in a time where people are more depressed and resigned from their lives than they've ever been.

We've been gifted with the unique ability to make the complex simple and tangible for everyday people desiring to change themselves for the better. In our work, we've found that the fear of not having or being enough prevents so many from seeing that they *already are* enough.

This book isn't going to stroke your ego and tell you that those ineffective patterns of yours are A-okay. It's not going to tell you that a few positive affirmations will get you to the life you've always dreamed of. No, this is a book that is going to meet you where you *really* are, challenge you to take yourself on, give you the tools to move through your life powerfully, and change the way you look at personal development forever. Big claim? Yes. But we'll stand behind it, because we've worked with thousands of people all over the globe who are living proof of this.

Do we promise that your life will be amazing every day after reading this book? No, life is impartial, and it will go on doing its life thing. The beautiful, the ugly, the profane, and the profound—life includes it ALL. The truth is, no one has a finite answer to the infinite nature of life. We don't know WHY certain things happen, and we can't explain and justify everything. However, we can show up to life's uncertainties in a powerful way, with tools that can help shape and create our reality.

So now that you know a little bit about *why* we wrote this book, let's jump into the pieces that will pull this whole thing together.

The first step is a reminder that you *always* have a choice. This part is all about awareness, and how with awareness, you have the key to unlock your inner greatness. We'll go into a few key distinctions that will give you the ability to really catch yourself in the act and get real about how you've been showing up to life. It all starts here, and if you can flex that awareness muscle, you can then create anything.

In the second step we'll dive into what it means to be *radically responsible*. We'll be exploring victim consciousness and the possibility that you may be creating, allowing, or perpetuating everything that is showing up in your experience. We'll also be opening up how the language you use is critical to your success in life.

Step 3 is all about *action*. It's a reminder that if you're committed to living a life of joy, abundance, and courage, then you must take *massive* action. In this chapter, we'll give you the tools to use in stressful, high-pressure situations, and we'll explore how to use your pain and ultimately turn it into power.

Some people play a role for so long that the role begins to play them. In step 4, "Own Who You Are," we'll dive deep into the importance of discovering your driving forces so you can get clear on what moves you, what it means to be transparent and live your truth, decoding why goals are BS, and how you can deal with comparison when it shows its ugly face.

And last but not least, we'll investigate what it means to really get the most out of life in step 5: "Have a Blast." In this chapter we'll give you our two cents on why fun is *critical* to living an epic life. We'll challenge you to break up your routines and shake things up so that you are able to experience what it feels like to be fully aligned with the truth of your being.

At the end of each chapter we've given you a "Short and Sweet" summary about what you just read, and we've noted the key phrases in "The Highlight Reel" (you're welcome!). We also finish each chapter with three "Powerful Questions" that you can ask yourself to see what emerges. We believe that powerful lives start by asking powerful questions!

A LITTLE HOUSEKEEPING

Being a know-it-all is annoying (we can relate because we both used to be one!). So before you jump in, we ask that you enter with a beginner's mind-set because you can't fill a cup that's already full. We love to sit in the question "What new possibilities are here for me?" even when we take the same courses or read the same book again and again. The truth is, you're a brand-new being every single moment—so create some space for new learnings, new insights, and new possibilities to develop by emptying your cup.

Once that cup is cleared, *commitment* comes next. You have to be willing to commit before you know the *how* or the *what* of your journey. It's like wanting to know how your child is going to turn out before you commit to having the kid in the first place. You have to commit to the journey and be willing to watch the *how* unfold as you go. Release your expectations about what your journey will look like or who you will become in the process of it. Just be present to what's coming up for you NOW.

So now that we've got that all squared away, go ahead and turn the page. We're excited to take this journey with you, so let's jump right in. Game on.

YOUR COMMITMENT

Any journey worth taking is worth showing up with 100 percent of yourself. We get that the work of living up to your highest potential can be challenging, confrontational, and altogether painful when you're really getting honest about yourself. It's certainly not always easy, but when we enter into this arena knowing that we are going to have some challenges to face, we can show ourselves a little grace throughout the process and remind ourselves of what's really important: *the commitment to ourselves.*

We invite you to take a moment and get clear on *why* you've picked up this book, *what* you're ready to break through, and why *now* is the time that it must happen. We invite you to get really grounded on what's possible for you to create throughout this journey, if you truly give it your all and play at 100 percent. Don't make this just *another* book—make this *the* book that changed everything.

MY COMMITMENT

1. I'm choosing to read this book because . . . (What do you desire more of? What are you calling in? What "gap" are you currently experiencing?)

2. I'm truly ready to break through . . .

3. I realize that the results I get out of this book are directly related to the effort that I put in. That being said, I know that in order to truly break through I will need to . . .

4. I deserve and commit to this journey because . . .

Thank you for truly taking yourself on. Thank you for saying YES to YOU so that the world can experience you in your magnificent fullness. We invite you to read this again and again, especially when you are faced with challenging times or find that you're bumping up against your own edges. This journey is uniquely yours, and you are here, now, right on time.

STEP 1

You Always Have a Choice

THE BRIDGE TO EMPOWERMENT

Between stimulus and response, there is a space. In that space is our power to choose our response. In our response lies our growth and our freedom.

—Viktor E. Frankl

YOU. ALWAYS. HAVE. A. CHOICE. No matter how bad it gets, no matter how low you feel, at any given moment you can choose something else.

We cannot intervene in a world we cannot truly see, and everyone is a world. The problem is, most people lack self-awareness. Cultivating an awareness of our patterns and habits is the beginning of radical, deep change, because with awareness comes *choice*. So many of us want change, growth, more money, respect, love, and connection, but we're not even aware of and honest about where we currently are, so we ultimately can't *choose* anything different. Put simply, if you can't *see* it, you can't *do anything* about it. And when you bring awareness to how you're showing up to life, you then have a choice. That choice is where your power lies.

Think of it like a map application on your phone. If you choose to go somewhere, you first have to let it know where you are so it can then chart the appropriate route. We were reminded of this when we first arrived in Bali to write this book. We were trying to locate a particular restaurant on our maps application in order to drive the scooter there, but the restaurant's name wasn't coming up. After cursing out our phone for a hot second, we suddenly realized that our phone's GPS thought we were still in Perth, Australia (the city we were previously in before coming to Bali). So we clicked the arrow to update the settings, which let it find where we currently were, and BOOM— the restaurant was found! In our own lives, the final address or dream that we're looking to get to already exists, but we have to know WHERE we're coming from *first* in order to find the most effective route to get us there.

Awareness is truly the key to all transformation because it's where we must start in order to then *choose* the best course for our lives. Awareness of self isn't always the easiest journey, either. We must be willing to take a good hard look in the proverbial mirror and get honest about how we're showing up to life. We must be willing to put in the work and be in the practice of catching our old beliefs, patterns, and agreements (our current operating system), even when we don't necessarily feel like it. This is about getting painfully honest about what has been and currently is running us so that we can intervene when we recognize our old, ineffective ways of being. Then we can choose something more effective for our lives and upgrade on the fly—sometimes before those old patterns pop up! Awareness of where we are (emotionally), who we're being in each moment, and what we're making things mean is where our true power lies.

Let it be known—building self-awareness isn't about judging or condemning ourselves (BAD YOU!), but rather about noticing what we've learned and picked up along our journey, then developing the ability to respond *differently* and create new habits. With the practice of the tools in this book, your awareness muscle will grow to such a deep and profound level that you'll begin to see yourself in an entirely different way (flex it, baby!).

HOW YOU DO ANYTHING IS HOW YOU DO EVERYTHING

One of the overarching principles we teach in our work is how you do *ANYTHING* is how you do *EVERYTHING*. This means that how you show up to something small and seemingly pointless in life is how you show up in all aspects of your life. The same pattern of self-sabotage that kicks in when you procrastinate on working out is the same self-sabotage that gets triggered when you're up for a promotion. Perpetually showing up late with your friends is mirroring the same lack of respect that you show for yourself.

It's all connected, and everything is touching everything; you cannot selectively be a particular way in one area of your life without it bleeding into and affecting other areas. So when you begin to flex those sexy awareness muscles of yours, you are able to take what you've noticed in one area of your life and see where else it's showing up—creating the space for exponential breakthroughs, growth, and new possibilities.

CONSCIOUS AND UNCONSCIOUS AGREEMENTS

One area to bring awareness to that we often don't think about is what unconscious agreements we're living by. Unconscious agreements are the beliefs or shoulds that go unexamined yet are secretly running the show (there is no choice when you're on autopilot!). These are the beliefs we picked up along the way from our family, society, institutions, friends, and partners that have shaped our view of the world. Most of us operate on the assumption that our beliefs, or agreements, are the RIGHT ones and that the world should meet our expectations of them.

DISAGREEMENT = Two opposing agreements (often unconscious) that do not align with each other.

If you're in any type of relationship (work, family, romantic, friends), our guess is you've probably experienced a disagreement at *least* once, if not a gazillion times! In relationships, most arguments are caused by our unconscious agreements clashing with someone else's. We decide other people are wrong for their way of not matching up to what we've unconsciously told ourselves is the "right" way to do things. Meanwhile, other people also fight to defend *their* way, which they unconsciously believe is the "right" way, too. In fact, most of the disagreements we get into are actually a product of two people with differing unconscious agreements, bumping up against each other, each trying to prove that *his or her* agreement is the way it *SHOULD* be. And as much as disagreements suck, the silver lining is that when we find ourselves in one (especially with those that we love), it's a beautiful opportunity to get conscious about our unconscious agreements so that we can choose to set a new agreement that works for the highest good of the relationship.

For example, Mark and Jackie disagree about how to handle the dishes. Jackie is frustrated that Mark has left his dirty dishes in the sink for more than two days (again!), allowing the old food to harden. Mark is agitated because he feels like this is no big deal; he was going to get to it *eventually*. In most cases, they would both argue their side until one or the other gave in; or worse, blow up at each other and not speak for a few days. But remember, this is an opportunity for *clarity*. If they chose to look at this as a chance to create a new sense of harmony in the relationship, things could look a lot different, and they could have more powerful choices than just arguments and frustration. Jackie could reflect on her unconscious agreement of washing the dishes immediately after use, which she automatically does because that's what was expected of her in her house growing up. Mark could reflect on his unconscious agreement about cleaning the house only once a week. While he doesn't mind a short-term mess, he certainly doesn't like it to build up over time because he grew up in a messy household that had no standards around cleaning.

Once they're clear about their unconscious agreements and where they originated from, they could figure out what they both CONSCIOUSLY choose and agree upon in the present moment that works for them both to create harmony. For instance, they could choose to come to an agreement that makes them both happy: Any dishes that aren't washed immediately will be soaked with water and soap until they are cleaned, avoiding the buildup of old food. Dishes will be left no longer than two days in the sink. Jackie agrees that she will continue to clean her own dishes immediately because she actually likes that habit; however, she will not worry about or stress over any of Mark's dirty dishes if he stays to the new conscious agreement.

In our relationship, we've made it our mission to bring as many unconscious agreements to the forefront as they come up, so we can choose to build a framework of conscious agreements that work for the highest good of *our* relationship. We've chosen conscious agreements around everything from how we handle laundry to how we are around the opposite sex; and any time a disagreement occurs, we recognize it as an opportunity to shed some light on an area of unconscious agreements we haven't yet discovered. Questioning old agreements deepens our understanding of ourselves and each other, and opens up the relationship for productive and blame-free communication. Amen to THAT.

UNCONSCIOUS BELIEFS BUILD OUR WORLD

Your unconscious agreements surprisingly reveal a lot about who you think you are, essentially shaping your reality. They bring to light your beliefs about the world and ultimately about yourself. They can leave you living life on default instead of living a life of your *choosing*.

If we asked you to finish the following prompts, you would potentially find some unexpected beliefs of yours that have likely gone unexamined for years. See what your initial response is to these prompts, and then ask yourself where that thought or belief may have originated from:

Women are . . . strong, providers, caring, nurturing

Men are . . . Simple minded,

The government is . . .

Indigenous people are . . . rightful dwellers of th. island

Asians are . . . nerdy, smart,

Americans are . . .

Money is . . .

My life is . . . Stuck -

We gave this to a client and what came out was very revealing:

Women are . . . beautiful, sexy, mothers, intense, crazy.

Men are . . . strong, providers, nonemotional, mean, competitive.

The government is . . . corrupt, cheaters, and liars.

Indigenous people are . . . victims, drunkards, outcasts.

Asians are . . . smart, cold, robotic, good at math.

Americans are . . . fat, sloppy, greedy, no culture.

Money is . . . the root of all evil, hard to get, always eluding me.

My life is . . . hard, stressful, fast-paced, boring, dull.

What he said *reveals* what he brings to his reality every time he encounters a person or situation that fits any of these descriptions. When he recognized that these unconscious agreements were affecting how he showed up in the world, he saw how they each created specific outcomes in his life. We then had him go through each one and get to the root of where it began. This awareness allowed him to understand why he attracted certain women, how he viewed manhood and other men, where his deep distrust came from, and how he is repelling both money and joy in his life. He began to see how these deep-rooted beliefs affected everything, and from this place of awareness, he had the *choice* to rewrite new, conscious agreements that felt more empowering and ultimately shifted his entire view of the world.

Use It Now

Uncovering what our deep-rooted beliefs are around certain areas unlocks the space to choose a new possibility for our experience of life. Now that we've given you the lowdown on unconscious agreements, see what comes up for you as you think about the following areas of relationships, money, and career. Once you uncover a few unconscious agreements or beliefs, try to pinpoint where you picked them up from, then decide what you choose *now*. Do you want to upgrade or shift this into a new agreement that fits into the life you are committed to creating? Or do you choose to stick with it because it feels effective for you?

UNCONSCIOUS AGREEMENT/BELIEF	WHERE YOU GOT IT FROM	NEW AGREEMENT
RELATIONSHIPS	RELATIONSHIPS	RELATIONSHIPS
Mean loss of independence Are forever	parents - 40 yrs. Fear of hurt/loss	Are 2 people loving each other unconditionally for any amant to grow and change as we do.
MONEY	MONEY	MONEY
Is a necessary evil	How I was raised Not abundant	Lets me do good things,
CAREER	CAREER	CAREER

CONDITIONED TENDENCIES/AUTOPILOT

How do you operate when shit hits the fan? How do you perform under pressure? When you're faced with a transition or change, what do you notice about your body and your reactions?

How we act in situations like these are called our conditioned tendencies (CTs). Traditionally, CTs consist of four main reactions: fight, flight, freeze, and appease. These are automatic patterns ingrained in us as to how we react to varying circumstances; these patterns are based on the environment we grew up in and how we've unconsciously trained ourselves or been trained by others. They are our default ways of being that arise when we're stressed-out, overtired, hungry, fearful, overwhelmed, or feeling attacked. They can appear as a physical reaction as well as thoughts and emotions. This isn't about how we would *like* to respond or react, but rather about what *actually* happens in the moment when we are caught off guard and the autopilot is operating.

When our CTs are in control, we have very little choice about how to respond to a situation (hello, reaction!!!). And quite frankly, if we want to kick ass in life and be way more effective, we've got to get off auto-pilot and jump into the driver's seat. The only way to not be a slave to our CTs and to create more space for choice and possibility to arise is to get clear about what our main CT is and see what triggers it in the first place.

Conditioned Tendencies

+ *Fight:* To push back or go against what is occurring.

+ *Flight:* To move away from something, to flee.

+ *Freeze:* To startle and stop dead in one's tracks (Cue: deer in headlights).

+ *Appease:* To try and neutralize the situation by moving toward it and being overly nice.

These automatic tendencies have been significantly influenced by our surroundings: from our individual experiences throughout the years, to our family and close relationships, to our local and global communities—the institutions we're a part of, societal norms and agreements—all the way to our relationship with something higher than ourselves. For example, the experience of growing up in a home filled with anger and fighting as an everyday thing would shape us differently than if we grew up in an environment where everyone was passive and would flee from their issues. The more awareness we bring to what shapes our CTs, the quicker we can move into transforming them, opening up more choice, possibilities, and powerful responses to the outside world as we grow.

Use It Now

Next time you're aware of yourself under pressure, triggered, or challenged, take a moment to notice how your autopilot shows up and reacts. (PS: Life is full of triggers, so this won't be too hard!) How do you react when someone cuts you off in traffic? What happens when your loved one challenges you or does something that sets you off? What do you notice about your reactions when you're under stress or are feeling overwhelmed? Remember, you're looking for whether you go into a conditioned tendency of fight, flight, freeze, or appease.

As you start to notice these CTs, you can begin to build new responses by taking a few deep breaths to bring yourself out of autopilot, and then consciously choosing a response that feels more empowering and effective. Each time you make a conscious choice to override the system, instead of just rolling on autopilot, you take your power back and flex those sexy awareness muscles of yours. This practice of choosing a different response is what ultimately builds a new "normal" for you.

DIMINISHERS

Have you ever noticed that RIGHT before a new opportunity or challenge develops, something happens inside? Let's say you get asked to share your thoughts at an important meeting. What happens? Maybe you hesitate to find ways to delay the inevitable. Or maybe you worry and stress out about what you're going to say and how it's going to land with the group—you want your response to be perfect so that you look good. Or maybe your mind flashes to all the things that could go wrong—how you should stand, where you should stand, and what you should say—your palms get sweaty, your throat closes up, and you feel sick to your stomach.

No matter what you may be faced with, when a new and unknown opportunity presents itself, we all have at least one diminisher that will show up. These nasty guys go to work on your confidence and interfere with your growth and your ability to take action—working directly for your ego to keep it safe AT ALL COSTS. They show up the minute we are asked to speak in public, learn something new, present an idea, or take on a big goal. The minute the smell of progress is in the air, these diminishers wake up and go to work on your subconscious mind, finding tricky ways to keep you small so your ego doesn't get hurt.

While many of us will resonate with quite a few of these, we all seem to have the BOSS of the entire diminisher crew—the one that, when everyone else is on lunch break, makes sure that he is there breaking down your self-belief, over and over again, right when you need it most. Take a look below at the usual suspects of diminishers and circle the one that is the BOSS of your inner squad:

+ *Procrastination:* This team member makes sure you don't do the thing you are asked to do or say you want to do because it believes that the longer you wait and put it off, the safer you'll be. When procrastination shows up, you'll suddenly find a million other reasons why you shouldn't act *now*. Instead of working on that big project of yours, procrastination will tap you on the shoulder and say it's probably a good time to research why armadillos have a hard shell or perhaps call your mother because you know that will take up an hour or so of your time. Another side of procrastination is waiting for others to go before you so they mess up FIRST, and you can hopefully learn from their mistakes and look a million times better than they did.

✦ *Perfectionism:* This overachiever loves for us to have everything perfect before we make any big moves. Perfectionism believes that if we can get everything done flawlessly, there is NO WAY the ego can get annihilated or judged. The problem with perfectionism is NOTHING will EVER be quite perfect enough, so this one usually tag-teams with its twin, procrastination, and waits and waits for the perfect moment—which usually never comes.

✦ *Overanalyzing:* This is the nerdy one of the group. Overanalyzing lives in the mind and loves to just bounce back and forth and back and forth and back and forth through

the canals of our brain, paralyzing us with a million different outcomes or strategies to win or not look bad. "We
should do it this way!" "Well, if we do it that way, then this
might happen!" "What if that happens? What will that
mean for me?" Overanalyzing loves for us to stay in the
world of ideas and theory so we never take actual ACTION.

✦ *Know-it-all:* The know-it-all of the group is a bit cocky
and inhibits our growth by whispering in our ear words
to the effect of "You already know this; you don't have to
do it again." Once she shows up, we are completely
closed off from new possibilities or new growth because
our cup is already full.

✦ *Criticizing:* Criticizing loves to tear down new ideas or
new opportunities presented to us. It often says things
like "This is dumb. Why would you want to do something like this, anyway?" Meanwhile he's completely terrified that we may get it wrong, so he banks on playing
Mr. Cool so there is no stake in the game in the first
place (a.k.a. nothing to lose).

✦ *Self-doubt:* Self-doubt has us giving up before we even
begin. She tells us that we're not good enough; we're
going to fail, or at best, mess it all up and look ridiculous.

She reminds us that we shouldn't even try if we know we're not going to be good at it in the first place.

✦ *Looking Good:* This prima donna loves to have us always looking good. She tells us that our self-worth is completely tied to our ability to impress others, so she will make sure we don't do anything that will have us looking stupid and messing up our image. She's SO concerned with the opinion of others that she makes sure that we're always "saving face," even at the cost of our own needs.

✦ *Not Asking for Help:* This team member loves to have us take it ALL on and do it all ourselves because then if it fails, we can place blame on the notion that we took on too much in the first place. He believes that the mere act of *asking* for help is absolute ego annihilation.

✦ *I Got This:* This eager beaver is the overconfident one of the crew who has us jumping in headfirst without even knowing what we're getting into. He has us showing up to opportunities underprepared with the justification that "I'll just wing it." His strategy is that if we don't put 100 percent of ourselves into it, we don't have that much to lose in the first place.

Use It Now

Now that you've been introduced to the crew of diminishers, take a moment and really think about which one is the head honcho of your mental house. Which one on the list resonated with you the most? Which one did you instantly recognize within yourself? Once you can spot them, you can see them for what they are (a strategy to keep your ego safe) and then *choose* to be bigger than them.

My BOSS diminisher is: _____

_____

Now that you've named it, next time it shows up, you can see the diminisher as a sign that progress is nearby (that's why they're there—to inhibit progress!) and choose to override the system. Ask yourself: "Am I more committed to staying safe and looking good, or am I more committed to my greatness?"

KEEP THIS IN MIND
WHEN YOUR DIMINISHER SHOWS UP

✦ *Procrastination:* Overwhelmed? Frustrated that you haven't done *one* thing from your list of a hundred? Easy tiger, do not fret; an effective way to override Procrastination is to focus on one small, tiny thing you can do *right now*, that will bring you closer to your desired outcome. Once you complete that one tiny thing, celebrate your tiny victory and then complete another. And step-by-step you'll begin to create a new pattern.

✦ *Perfectionism:* Standards set so high that they're out of reach and impossible to get to? The first thing to understand, if *this* is your boss diminisher, is that not a single human being is "perfect"—and it's highly unlikely that you'll actually be the first perfect one! (Whew!) Once you drop the impossible standard of perfection, you can then sit in the question: "What would be *good enough* right now?" Another gentle reminder for yourself is to focus on the ride rather than the destination. (The ride is the fun part, anyway!)

✦ *Overanalyzing:* Debilitated with all the options? Feeling stressed by all that things that could go right *and* wrong? Worried you'll make the wrong decision and regret it the rest of your life? Overanalyzing is often about staying in the question to keep us from taking action, so remind yourself that no matter which action you choose, *you truly cannot fail.* No matter the result, you'll learn and you'll grow—but you have to take *some action* first. So ask yourself "What am I committed to?" Then let your commitment be your internal compass to guide you into your next move.

✦ *Know-it-all:* Tired of pretending? Let go, it's okay for you not to have it under control. The most effective way to override your inner know-it-all is to remind yourself that if anything in nature is not growing, it's dying. And by living with the idea that you already "know" it all, there is no room to *grow* at all. A question to ask yourself when you see this diminisher pop up is: "What is new for me to learn here or to take deeper?"

✦ *Criticizing:* Hi, stop it! Stop pretending like you don't care. When this diminisher shows up, ask yourself, "What am I afraid of right now?" When you can get honest with yourself about your fears, you can then choose to override them and be more open to new possibilities and learning.

✦ *Self-doubt:* Psst . . . your higher-self asked us to remind you that out of the seven billion people on the planet there is only one you, and that you're freaking amazing. Overriding Self-doubt takes a willingness to tap into the deeper meaning of what you're about to do and make it all about *that,* instead of all about *you.* It's not about you, it's about the message, or meaning that you are here to help initiate. Another helpful tip is to lovingly remind yourself that there is nothing that has been put in front of you that you are not equipped to handle.

✦ *Looking Good:* Hello gorgeous! Guess what, you already are amazing and you already are smoking hot because there is only one incredible YOU! So something to keep in mind when "Looking Good" shows up, is that *no one* is quite as concerned with you as you may think. Most people are in their own minds worrying about what *you* think about *them.* Ask yourself, "How would I show up in this situation if I knew no one was watching?" and do *that.*

✦ *Not Asking for Help:* Tired of doing it all yourself yet? Overwhelmed and resentful for all those "things" you feel you *have* to do? Well, in order to truly tackle this diminisher, you must first truly get that nothing in this world is a solo act. Supporting others is often something that people cherish being able to do, and to rob them of that gift is like a rejection of their love. So ask yourself, "How can I ask for and receive support in this moment?"

✦ *I Got This:* No you don't. Ha! Seriously, you don't. When you catch yourself in this diminisher, diving into something again without truly understanding what you're getting yourself into, stop, take a deep breath, and just wait. Don't make any brash decisions—simply listen and observe, and then after you've thought about what it is you're actually committing to for at least, but not limited to, five minutes, then make a decision.

DEATH TO RIGHT AND WRONG

At the root of ALL these diminishers is the need to be right, to look good, and to keep us safe from failing (and frankly, looking like an idiot). Right and wrong, good and bad—these are mental constructs that keep us small and hold us back. In order to play full-out in life, we need to obliterate these constructs and reframe them to more powerful paradigms.

CONSTRUCT	REFRAME
Right/Better	Effective
Wrong/Worse	Not effective
Good	It works for me
Bad	It doesn't work for me

Now, as simple as this linguistic tool may seem, it's a COMPLETE game changer. It has single-handedly changed the way we operate within our business and with our friends and family, while also transforming the quality of our relationship with each other. Removing these constructs takes blame out of the equation and invites a more open and expanded view of the situation, ultimately creating more possibilities (more possibilities mean more epic life to be had!). And let's not forget the most important place this tool is used—with ourselves!!! We tend to be so incredibly hard on ourselves, judging our actions with these constructs of right/wrong/good/bad, which can stop us dead in our tracks and be a killer of our self-esteem. So it's time to nix the negativity and opt for a more *effective* approach. (See? We used one right there!)

RESISTING OR ALIGNING

At the heart of most of our suffering as human beings is a resistance to what *is*—a longing for life to be different in some way. Arguing with reality is like being pissed off at your dog for not being able to do your taxes. You can try to train your dog day in and day out to be the best accountant in the world, but at the end of the day he will still bark and lick your feet (and will probably be pretty terrible with a calculator). Whether it's wishing that the weather was different or that someone we loved didn't leave or hurt us, there's no point in resisting what is. In fact it is this resistance to what is that causes suffering in life. Your power lies in aligning with and accepting life in all its glory and declaring a new possibility from that place of acceptance. Point-blank: the more you argue with and resist what is, the more you suffer.

We live in Los Angeles, California, which is filled with palm trees. One of the most amazing things about palm trees is how they sway with the smallest breeze. Standing tall above the city streets, they align with the wind, and let the breeze sway them back and forth, while their trunks stay rooted to the ground below. The palm tree never resists the wind; it never fights against what is. So no matter how rough the winds get, the palm accepts the breeze and remains flexible to life, knowing that in time even the strongest winds will subside. Imagine if palm trees resisted and fought against the wind, remaining immovable and rigid—they would quickly snap in half because of all the stress that resistance would create.

Most of us create unnecessary stress and suffering in life because we resist what is. We stand firm and stubborn, refusing to be flexible with life's breeze, holding on to the notion that life SHOULD be in accordance with our beliefs (No wind! No wind! No wind!). If we want to feel more flow in life, we must all learn to align with the wind, like the palm tree. No matter where you are on your journey, whether it be in a light breeze or in a freaking hurricane that feels like it will never pass, when you choose to accept and align with it (looking for the beauty, lessons, possibilities, and ways in which you participated) your life will be radically shifted; you'll feel a sense of ease and grace even when you're in the heaviest of storms.

Now, it's important to note that while we can't always change external circumstances immediately, we can always change things within ourselves. So the key is to accept what is from the external world and then go to work shifting and adjusting what we are able to change within our internal world to create more harmony. And a powerful way that we can begin to make massive shifts within ourselves is by obtaining feedback.

FEEDBACK

Michael Jordan, one of the most well-known athletes on the planet, had a shooting coach. Now, why would a six-time NBA champion, ten-time NBA All-Star, and Olympic gold medalist rely on someone else's feedback about his amazing shooting? After all, he is one of the best in the world and doesn't necessarily *need* anyone telling him what to do. But that is exactly what makes him—or anyone else living an extraordinary life, for that matter—get such powerful results. Extraordinary people like Michael Jordan are addicted to the areas of their lives within their careers, relationships, or performances that they can't see; they love to learn more about what they don't know so that they can adjust, grow, and create a massive edge in life, ultimately becoming the best versions of themselves.

No matter who we are or what level of life we're playing at, we all have room for growth and improvement, and this is where the work of feedback comes in. Most people try to avoid feedback as much as possible because they decide that feedback means that they're not good enough (major slap to the ego!). And let's be clear here: feedback is NOT judgment, criticism, law, or absolute truth; it's simply someone else's *experience* of you.

Some feedback won't resonate, while some may sting a bit, because some part of you knows it's true. But whether you actively seek feedback from a coach or friends, or simply look at the feedback called your life, it's always there, regardless of whether you choose to acknowledge it or not. The truth is, if you're really committed to living an incredible life, you've got to become best friends with your blind spots. You must be courageous enough to look at the areas of your life that need development or work, be willing to shift and grow in those areas, and be consistent with this practice. This means getting uncomfortable, hearing things you don't want to hear (but secretly already knew), and being humble enough to incorporate this information instead of instantly being defensive and trying to remain "right" about your life. This constant commitment to growth is truly what separates the ordinary from the extraordinary in life, and it's readily available to all of us if we *choose* to take it on.

In our work we have people reach out to loved ones and ask them for specific and targeted feedback. This is all about seeing a reflection of who you are through the eyes of those who know you best. Feedback can be uncomfortable, but it's necessary in order to gain insight into how you show up to other people, so that you can consciously choose to grow into who you desire to be. You may be INTENDING to show up a certain way (as loving, a good listener, and patient), but you may be coming off completely different from how you intended (like a total asshole). And since we can't know how other people experience us, the *only* way to uncover what our potential blind spots are is to get a direct, brutally honest view from someone else. As you continue the feedback process with multiple people, look for patterns that show up again and again—that's where the gold of your self-growth lies.

Alexi's Story

When I first began the process of feedback nearly ten years ago, I was terrified. I spent my entire life avoiding any sort of criticism or opinions from others because my self-image was far too fragile to be rocked in any way. I had built up what I thought was an incredible facade that I had it "all together" and everything was "perfect." Doing feedback interviews instantly shattered that concept, when my friends and family could see past all the BS I thought I had covered up so well. But that's not even the most important thing I learned. The most powerful revelation I received came when I asked one of my best friends and business partner in my nonprofit for feedback. To put it gently, she was reluctant and didn't want to participate in my feedback interview. She politely asked me to do it with someone else and eventually came clean that she feared I would hold it against her and would hate her for it. THIS WAS THE BEST FEEDBACK I HAD GOTTEN. The fact that my best friend and business partner didn't feel safe telling me how I showed up to her instantly revealed to me that I must be showing up as defensive and righteous—always wanting to "win." This was incredible feedback for me, and I began to look at all areas of my life and saw that I did this with everyone I was close to. I fought tooth and nail for my way to be the "right" way and got incredibly defensive and resentful when someone challenged me.

In sharing this massive breakthrough with my partner, I revealed a level of humility to her that she had never experienced from me before. Once she saw this new side of me, she agreed to do the feedback interview because she could see that I truly was committed to growth. That interview left me so inspired and with so much ammunition for my growth that I decided to interview my two ex-boyfriends, whom I had shared a significant part of my life with. It was fascinating (and not all that surprising!) that the feedback I received was all the same: I was defensive, closed off, self-righteous, and stubborn as hell.

Did it sting a little? Hell yes. I didn't like it because deep down I realized that they were seeing what I thought no one could see; and that's exactly why I KNEW something had to shift. I really was ready to take myself on in an incredible way and get to work on my blind spots so I could build powerful relationships with others and, most important, with myself. I knew I had a big life that was waiting for me . . . and I knew that in order to call it in, I had to be ready for it.

Preston's Story

When I first began this process I was amazed and completely pissed off about what came back in my feedback conversations. Over and over and over again people called me "closed off." As you can imagine, my ego was not very happy about this and it wanted me to retreat and isolate even more. "Who *the hell do they think they are? They don't even know me, I'm not f'n closed off!" Ha! What a joke! I was totally keeping everyone at a distance to keep myself safe. And when I chose to face, accept, and align with that feedback, my entire life shifted. I dug a bit deeper and tracked down where the pattern began and started the journey of catching it in the act . . . and to be honest, I'm STILL catching it (flexing that awareness muscle!).*

Feedback is a never-ending process, and it's happening even when we may not be aware of it. What's currently in your bank account is feedback. Your relationship status is feedback. How your partner treats you is feedback. It's all feedback. Your job is to welcome the feedback because it points to an area that you can improve on and a possible blind spot that you weren't aware of. When we can catch our blind spots, we can intercept our old patterns and *choose* to create new, more empowering ones. Remember, it's not about good or bad, right or wrong; it's about building awareness around what patterns and blocks are effective or not effective for your life and knowing that you always have a choice of what you can do next.

Use It Now

CONDUCT YOUR OWN FEEDBACK INTERVIEW

Reach out to someone you are really close to and ask him or her the questions that follow. Don't respond with any reasons, excuses, defensiveness, explanations, or expressions; simply thank that person. Be sure to tell your interview subject that you are ready and willing for honest feedback and will be responding only with gratitude (no matter how uncomfortable the feedback makes you!). And if the feedback is all positive and he or she can't offer *any* constructive criticism, then that's feedback, too! It's feedback that you may not be in the space for honest feedback! Remember, there is always room for improvement!

SAMPLE OPENING SCRIPT

Hi! I need your opinion on something, if you have ten minutes to spare?

I'm entering a new phase in my life and part of my commitment is to discover what my blind spots are so that I can really fine-tune the areas in my life that have been holding me back. All I need from you is your honesty.

Just to let you know, I'm not able to respond with anything but a thank-you. Know that I am doing this for my highest growth, so I really do want you to feel like you can be open and honest with me; that's how I will get the most out of this.

And if everything you say is super-nice, I'll know you're lying to me! Can I count on you to be honest, even if you think it will hurt my feelings?

Great! Let's do this! First question . . .

Feedback Interview

How would you describe me in three words?

_____

_____

_____

What would you say are three of my strengths?

_____

_____

_____

What would you say are three areas that I could improve on?

_____

_____

_____

_____

_____

What three things do you LOVE about how I am with you in our relationship?

_____

_____

_____

_____

When it comes to our relationship, what could I be better at or improve on?

_____

_____

_____

_____

What would you say are my ineffective patterns that I may not be aware of?

_____

_____

_____

_____

_____

What would you say is the single biggest thing holding me back from my greatness?

_____

_____

_____

_____

_____

THE SHORT AND SWEET

We cannot intervene in a world we cannot see; and bringing awareness to our operating system is the beginning of radical, deep change, because with awareness comes *choice*. When we bring awareness to our agreements, conditioned tendencies, diminishers, blind spots, and things we're in resistance to, we can then *choose* to show up differently. It takes exceptional courage and humility to face off with ourselves, but this is what truly separates the ordinary from those who lead incredible, extraordinary lives.

THE HIGHLIGHT REEL

✦ When you bring awareness to how you're showing up to life, you then have a choice, and that choice is where your power lies.

✦ How you do *anything* is how you do *everything*.

✦ Most disagreements happen because both parties involved are fighting for *their* way, because it is what they unconsciously believe is the "right" way, or the way life *should* be. Banish right/wrong, good/bad, and better/worse from your vocabulary. These words block our choice and possibility and set us up for judgment and blame.

✦ In high-stress situations, we all have a conditioned tendency that will kick in. When we can identify ours, we can catch it before it gets out of hand and choose something that feels more effective in the moment.

+ Any time we have the opportunity for progress or expansion, we have a team of diminishers who will show up and attempt to keep our ego safe. Catching these diminishers in action gives us the opportunity to override them and choose what we're more committed to.

+ When we align with what IS in life, rather than resist it, we create more ease and flow.

+ Becoming aware of our blind spots through feedback is an incredible tool for exponential growth.

POWERFUL QUESTIONS

1. In what ways do I fight to be *right* about my beliefs/agreements?

2. What about life am I in resistance to?

3. What am I pretending not to know?

STEP 2

Be Radically Responsible

THE BRIDGE TO GETTING UNSTUCK

With great power comes great
responsibility.
—Voltaire

ow that you've learned about step 1 for creating a kick-ass life, we get to dive into what we refer to in our work as the glue: radical responsibility. Cool phrase, but what does it even mean?

We hear the term "responsibility" used over and over again in countless new age, self-help, and leadership books, but few people actually practice the full embodiment of this word. By definition, responsibility means the state of being accountable to and for something. Sounds easy enough, right? Yeah, sure, it's easy to say you need to be 100 percent responsible for your life, but this can be much harder to actually implement and practice. Why? Because we've been trained since we were young to blame others for our pain: the friend who stole your toy, the parent who left the family, the ex who cheated on you, the government that screwed you over, and the employers who never knew how good they had it.

Hence the word "radical." The dictionary likes to define this word as "far-reaching or thorough," and we like to say it means you are so ridiculously unreasonable about your commitment to responsibility that it's insane, it's borderline obsessive, and it's absolutely rigorous. This requires some heavy-duty lifting, but remember *you asked* for an epic life, and this is what it takes. So yes, this means you take ALL OF LIFE ON. Yes, this means you are the creator of your reality. Yes, this also means that you caused, allowed, perpetrated, or participated in co-creating everything you're currently experiencing. This includes (but is not limited to) every disagreement you've ever had, every trauma you've experienced, every limiting belief pattern you've been in, and even the state of the world. Is this radical? Hell yes! But it takes responsibility that is so absolutely, insanely radical to ACTUALLY make a shift in your life, and ultimately, the world.

We get that this can be extremely triggering for some. "What do you mean, we're responsible for it ALL? What about being cheated on? Is that MY fault? What about innocent children who are the victims of heinous crimes? Are THEY responsible for that? What about famine or war? What about the state of our environment? How can I and WHY should I be responsible for it all?" Hold your horses—we're getting to that. (Keep reading!)

This isn't to say that we are responsible for all the incredibly sucky events happening in our life: it rains on our wedding day, we lose a child, or we experience major loss when a natural disaster strikes. The truth is, terrible things do happen. And pain in life is inevitable, but *suffering* is a CHOICE. When we choose radical responsibility, we choose the empowering *perspective* that we are responsible for *our experience* of the event—no matter how undesirable or beautiful it may be. We can choose the experience of fear, doubt, and blame, or we can choose to release blame altogether and choose the experience of a new perspective, a lesson, a gift, or perhaps a deepening of how we know ourselves and the world. In the situations we can't control, we can control how we respond to them.

Taking radical responsibility is a critical step in creating a life of our own design instead of living a life of default. And in order to design an amazing life, we must be willing to focus on what we desire RIGHT NOW, instead of constantly running away from, resisting, or blaming our past. Radical responsibility starts with radical *acceptance* of people, circumstances, and situations as they are. Acceptance is a knowing that all is perfect right now, no matter how it may appear on the surface. Anything other than that is being in RESISTANCE to reality (and that's a dead end). Once we've accepted what IS, we can move into seeing the role we've played in what we're currently experiencing.

As we mentioned in chapter 1, most people have an unconscious belief that there's a way the world should and shouldn't be, and hold those "should"s as RIGHT. But as long as we hold our "should"s as law or absolute truth, we are setting ourselves up for suffering, because life doesn't play in "should"s, it just IS, and it's unapologetically impartial. When life does its impartial "life" thing, most of us tend to get all cranky because the world didn't adjust to our beliefs. We continue to blame the world, play the victim, and place the responsibility completely outside of ourselves to make us feel better. Let's be clear, radical responsibility is not faultfinding or blaming ourselves instead—that's STILL blame and still based on considering that life SHOULD be a certain way. Remember, life doesn't play in "should"s, so it's futile to try to control the world into what works for us. Instead, we can look at all of life as our teacher and begin asking ourselves: "What could I choose instead?"

PAIN IN LIFE IS NOT OPTIONAL. PERPETU-ATING THAT PAIN IS.

We don't suffer in life because life is so unfair and unpredictable, but rather because we are attached to our idea of the way life SHOULD be and hold tightly to those expectations. This deserves restating: Life is impartial. It's constantly in a state of flux and change. When we stop trying to control it and accept what IS, we free up loads of energy for us to be more effective (and more awesome). However, we can't just accept the "good" parts of life, because that's just the half of it—we must be willing to accept ALL of life. A destructive tsunami or the death of a child is just as much a part of life as new love or beautiful scenes in nature. We must be willing to accept and honor both beginnings and endings, light and dark, birth and death. Everything is included; it is ALL life.

You alone hold the key to your personal freedom, and it begins with accepting all of what IS. We believe that the moment you get that you're the author, the source, and the painter of the masterpiece of your experience, you can radically shift into a state that you could've never imagined possible.

BEING A VICTIM VERSUS VICTIM CONSCIOUSNESS

There is a difference between those who are victims to something outside of their control and those who hold victim consciousness around an event.

You can be an actual victim to an event in life—such as a rape or molestation, a natural disaster, or an accident. There are some things that are so far beyond what we can comprehend that we can't even begin to explain WHY they happened. However, in this present moment, we do have the power to show up and choose a new perspective on what happened in the past, and it begins with a shift in our state of mind.

For instance, people who were molested at a young age absolutely had something occur to them; they were a victim to a particular set of circumstances. Now, they could do what most of the world does and choose to hold victim consciousness around the event, allowing the pain and trauma from their past to dim their light and hold them back in life. Or that same person could choose an empowered, radically responsible attitude and be done feeling victimized by the circumstance. She could operate from radical responsibility and know that, as an adult, she no longer wants to PERPETUATE the event or to live in the disempowering stories and patterns that resulted from it, choosing to see the gifts that came from it and ultimately forgiving the person who assaulted her.

CATALYST MOMENTS

We understand that some events in our past seem so completely insurmountable and painful that we feel we can't possibly find the gift in them or choose to forgive; however, this is precisely where your opportunity for expansion lies. These painful memories are catalyst moments because they are often the point at which we make one of two choices: either we continue to stay in victim consciousness and allow this event to sabotage our joy and greatness in life, OR we use it as the moment that changes everything, as fuel to ignite and catapult ourselves into the life of our dreams. Catalyst moments are choice points, the moments that shake us up and wake us up. Often our greatest pain disturbs us enough to act as a wake-up call from our comfort zones;

it forces us to reexamine everything. Often it's not until the storm really hits that we realize what was rooted in our lives and what wasn't. Sometimes we have to be knocked off the path to realize that we were never on the right one in the first place. And let us lovingly remind you that there is nothing on your plate that you can't handle.

Alexi's Story

One of my biggest catalyst moments in life came out of a truly traumatic event. When I was around twenty years old I was sexually assaulted and raped. What transpired in that event truly shook me to my core, and for years I decided to bury it deep in the back of my mind, hoping that the pain would eventually go away if I pretended that it had never happened. For six years, I stuffed it down and put all my energy and focus into building "success" in my life and doing everything I could to keep any sort of pain or vulnerability out. I built a brick wall (one that would've given the Great Wall of China a run for its money!) to keep out pain, but it also kept out joy, gratitude, love, and happiness. One day, during one of my yearly service trips to Africa with my organization, E.P.I.C., my partner Tennille and I experienced a beautiful moment. We had just drilled a clean-water well in this particular village, and all the women had come out to celebrate and show us gratitude with song, dance, and prayer. I saw that Tennille was moved to tears as this amazing woman named Zambda looked at us and spoke with so much praise and joy in her voice, but I also noticed that I couldn't feel much of anything. Logically, I was incredibly proud and grateful to have been able to serve in that way, but I couldn't actually experience or *feel* any of that joy and love and actually let it land in my body. This sparked my journey inward and eventually led me to find that I had built a brick wall that kept all those beautiful emotions out. This work allowed me to see that I let the trauma fester deep within me. Perpetuating my pain created a massive disconnection from and distrust of others because I wasn't willing to access and confront this dark event in my life. And finally, I learned that with true forgiveness I could cultivate two qualities without which I wouldn't be able to do the work I do today: compassion and empathy. Now I am able to truly BE with people who have experienced enormous amounts of pain and suffering, because I know what it's like to be at the depths of my own humanity. Without that experience, there is no way I would be able to do the type of work I feel so honored to be able to do with people from all over the world who have been through their own traumas. This moment became instrumental in *sparking the unfolding of my purpose; it completely knocked me off the path I was on and opened up incredible new possibilities for me.*

CREATE, ALLOW, PERPETUATE

No matter what your level of involvement was with an event, you were there and you were a part of it; therefore, you participated in some way, shape, or form. And when we acknowledge the role we play in each situation, we then have the power to shift it.

We teach that each person is responsible for his or her 100 percent participation in every event. This means that if there are three people involved, 300 percent needs to be accounted for, and 100 of that 300 percent is YOURS to claim, regardless of how big or small the event was. Perhaps you never said anything or you continue to hold onto the pain and resentment of what transpired to this present day. This concept is easier to understand in situations like our relationships with a partner, friends, coworkers, or family members; but can we be 100 percent responsible for our part in the state of the world that we are living in? This would mean that there is 700 BILLION percent responsibility to be accounted for, but guess what? You're a part of that, and your 100 percent responsibility may be as subtle as your being too focused on the problem and not on the solution, or that the hate and judgment that still lives within you is a reflection of the same hate and judgment that's occurring throughout the world. Goethe said it best: "Let everyone sweep in front of his own door, and the whole world will be clean."

By sitting in the question "How did I either create, allow, or perpetuate this event?" you can step fully into your power by stepping fully into radical responsibility. For some situations, you may find that you cross over into a couple of the domains below, and in others you may resonate with only one, but use this as a guide to support you in taking the often challenging step into your own radical responsibility.

CREATE

It's our belief that creation happens on many levels, some not so visible to the untrained eye. We teach that creating an event or circumstance can mean you were the "SPACE" for the event to occur. This means that you created the environment for something to grow into what eventually became the circumstance.

A great example of this that we can look to is with relationships. Let's say Partner A cheats on Partner B. On the surface, most would side with Partner B and fault Partner A for what he or she did. But how did Partner B help CREATE this? Perhaps Partner B was too focused on the kids or on work and took the relationship for granted, not making quality time a priority. Partner B could look at this act of cheating and be in total victim consciousness by blaming it all on Partner A, and holding it over the other person's head for a lifetime. Or Partner B could take radical responsibility for the situation and recognize that he or she played just as big a role in helping to create an *environment* for cheating by ultimately neglecting the relationship. Now, this does not absolve Partner A of any responsibility in the situation, but it does open up the possibility for authentic communication and a powerful resolution.

Another great example is people who consume processed and packaged food from the grocery store for most of their adult lives. If you take into consideration the chemicals, sugars, and preservatives found in these foods, people who choose to eat such foods on a consistent basis could have helped bring about their cancer, heart disease, or diabetes. Based on their choices, they created the ENVIRONMENT for disease to occur.

It is our belief that the CONTEXT determines the CONTENT, or the quality of the soil determines the condition of the tree; and we create our CONTEXT by the choices we make or don't make on a moment to moment basis. (We'll dive deeper into this distinction in chapter 4.)

ALLOW

Accepting that we allowed events to happen is sometimes the hardest thing to take radical responsibility for. These are the ones with red warning flags all over them, yet we STILL allowed the situation to happen. Common examples of allowing are: staying with someone who is routinely abusive; staying in a job that doesn't serve you; eating, drinking, and drugging yourself into a particular state of health; not speaking up when we feel compelled to; and even buying things that noticeably diminish our bank accounts or the environment. It's the small actions that we sometimes allow over and over again that eventually add up to a reality that doesn't sit well for us.

What you PERMIT, you PROMOTE. This can be one of the subtlest and most pervasive things because it's all in the details. For example, it's in the inappropriate jokes that your dad cracks every Thanksgiving that you never hold him accountable for, until one day he goes too far and you decide never to speak to him again. It's the 400-calorie coffee with whipped cream you get every morning on your way to work that eventually turns into a spare tire around your waist. It's not saying how you really feel to "keep the peace" in your relationship until one day that turns into an explosive fight where you've had enough. Often we blame our unfavorable results on people or circumstances outside of us, instead of looking at how we've allowed it to get to this point in the first place. However, when we get radically responsible for our lives, we can all find countless ways for which we've allowed our reality to manifest bit by bit.

PERPETUATE

You know that old hurt that you're still hanging on to? Oh, come on, you know, the one that you're "so over," but when you see that person or hear his name, you cringe a little inside and lash out with a not-so-friendly statement about him? Well, that's a form of PERPETUA-TION. When we PERPETUATE an event, we hold on to anger, resentment, hurt, frustration, sadness, shame, guilt, fear, or yearning in hopes that holding on to it will somehow make it go away. (Or maybe we secretly hope perpetuating it will create some justice and uneasiness for the person we haven't forgiven yet!) But stewing in your own anger, hurt, or frustration doesn't solve any-thing; it just perpetuates the pain.

Forgiveness is an enormous part of radical respon-sibility because choosing forgiveness means we must be willing to operate from a place of personal power. Now, let's be clear, forgiveness doesn't mean that you're absolving others or pardoning their offense; for-giveness is about coming to terms with and accepting WHAT IS, and then choosing to release that poison from your life.

A beautiful way to illustrate this is with a story. Two men, let's call them Jake and Dan, are out in the wilder-ness on an epic hiking trip. All of a sudden they both get bitten on the leg by a deadly snake, which slithers off in a hurry after the encounter. Jake pulls out his knife and goes straight after the snake, chasing it deep into the jungle. On the other hand, Dan pulls out his knife and goes straight into his leg, carving out the area that the poison has infiltrated, and proceeds to suck the poison out. Because Jake was focused on punishing the snake, he let that poison seep deeper and deeper into his bloodstream, allowing it to slowly kill him. Dan chose to focus on the poison that was inside of him, and because of that he's still alive to this day.

While this is just a story, it's a beautiful illustration of how most of us handle "poison" in our lives. Someone does something to us (the snake comes in for a bite), and then we spend our entire lives hating, blaming, and chasing that snake for justice; meanwhile, a deep poison dwells within us that is slowly breaking down our vitality and livelihood. (And we see this in such a literal way when we see someone who is incredibly bitter, resentful, and hardened by life.) That is the product of PERPETUATION.

When we go to the SOURCE of the issue within ourselves, cut out the poison, and see why it hurt so bad, we can clear it. Often one person's actions are simply lighter fluid to a whole set of sparks that lived within you before you even knew the person who poured the fluid! That's why the same event can happen to two different people, and each will have a different response to it. One person may be traumatized and totally in victim consciousness around it, while the other person can simply shrug it off. It's because the spark didn't exist within him or her in the first place, so the lighter fluid didn't have the same explosive impact. Just imagine the amount of energy that would be freed up if we didn't use it to blame someone else. So how do we forgive something that seems so unforgivable?

Use It Now

THE FORGIVENESS PROCESS

1. *Acceptance:* First, we have to know that forgiveness doesn't take two people; it just takes YOU. And you have to really be ready to get all that yucky poison out of your system (no resentment and bitterness for me, thank you!).

2. *Radical Responsibility:* Second, think about what sparks were within you in the first place that the other person's lighter fluid may have ignited. Perhaps it was a deep-rooted insecurity, or perhaps it's not feeling worthy. Whatever spark was ignited is the work that YOU still get to do with yourself.

3. *Compassion:* Third, consider the pain the other person may currently be in. Hurt people hurt people, so take a moment and feel some deep compassion for what that person might be going through or may have been through for him or her to behave in this way.

4. *Love and Gratitude:* Finally, send the person love and gratitude for bringing a deeper awareness to what still lies within you that's calling to be cleared. Every person and circumstance is a teacher for us.

It's important to know that forgiveness is a process that doesn't necessarily happen overnight. So if you find yourself stuck, stop for a moment and show some compassion and grace toward yourself for being will-ing to be in the process. No matter how long ago that snake may have bit you, or how far into the jungle you went chasing it, you always have the choice to pull out that knife and start getting to work on removing the poison.

EVERYONE AND EVERYTHING ARE YOUR TEACHERS

Everyone and every situation are your teachers (especially those that annoy you most!).

The person who screwed you over, the hurricane that obliterated your home, the results that came back not so favorable—they are all there for us to rise above and expand into the greatness we are here for. When we look at our lives from this perspective, we open up incredible learning opportunities for our highest growth. Often, without that person or situation, we wouldn't have that priceless insight that allows us to take a deeper look into ourselves. So when you're faced with a triggering moment, some questions you could ask yourself are:

+ What wouldn't I have been able to understand or develop without this circumstance or person?

+ What about this person or situation am I judging or resisting? How am I judging or resisting that part of myself?

✦ How is this illuminating a possible pattern or habit I have been unwilling to look at?

✦ In what way is this feedback for my life?

✦ How is this grooming me to be stronger and to handle more in my life?

LANGUAGE

When it comes to radical responsibility, one of the most important places to practice it is with our language.

Our power as humans to literally create our own reality begins with our words. And just as our words are building blocks, they can also be weapons of mass destruction. No matter how you slice it, you're always using your words to advance your beliefs and ideas into reality. By choosing to move into radical responsibility with your language, you will make more conscious choices in how to express yourself and will ultimately design a life of your creation. We have found that there are four important aspects to be aware of when it comes to using radically responsible language: integrity, language upgrades, stories, and complaining.

INTEGRITY

Sure, we all know it's important to keep our word, but how many of us actually *do* it?

Having integrity with your word is not just about having integrity with promises made to others; it's also about keeping the promises we make to ourselves. It's easier to keep our promises to those we love or care about, or perhaps when our job, money, or reputation is on the line. But can we keep our word to ourselves when no one is watching? Can we not eat that piece of chocolate that is staring us in the face even though we promised to cut out sugar? Can we go to the gym on a cold and rainy day because we told ourselves we would, even when we don't feel like it? We can't be in full radical responsibility with our language until we're willing to have integrity in ALL areas of our lives. And the hard truth is, the more we break our promises to ourselves, the less weight our words hold. They lose their creative juice and powers because there is never any real follow-through on them. The idea here is to keep your word as if your life depended on it, because in some ways, it does. Again, our words are our greatest superpower; they can build an entirely different reality or demolish one all in the same breath. So when we don't harness the true power of our words by keeping them, we diminish their effectiveness and basically hand in our magical sword and cape for a life of dull default.

Keeping Our Word with Others

We're not going to beat you over the head with this one, but we do want to point out something important: YOU ARE ALWAYS TEACHING PEOPLE HOW TO BE WITH YOU.

Do you have people in your life who are ALWAYS late? (If you can't think of a friend, it may be *you*!) The first couple of times, you forgave them. But after a while you started showing up later because you knew they weren't going to keep their word about being on time. You started inviting that person out less and less, deciding to drive your own car (so you weren't waiting on them . . . again!), and you eventually didn't want to hang out with them because you felt blatantly disrespected. Sooner or later, that breach of trust with a "small" thing like being on time starts to bleed out all over your relationship. "How can I trust them with anything if I can't even trust them to show up on time?" Your late friend has time and again taught you how to be with him. And just as that person is teaching you how to respect and be with him, YOU are teaching those around you how to respect and be with you.

So if you think no one is noticing your little white lies, think again. If you think no one cares about your incessant lateness, you're mistaken. If you think no one is taking note of all your empty promises, you're delusional! And again, this isn't about right or wrong, but be honest—HOW IS THIS WORKING OUT FOR YOU?

Your word is all you have when it comes to developing self-respect and trust and honor with others. You want to live a powerful life beyond measure? Clean up your act and start being your word.

Gossip

Whether it's at the office cooler or from your favorite magazine or TV show, from this point forward, consider "gossip" a dirty word. Plain and simple, when you gossip, it has to come through YOU first, and all that negativity leaves a nasty residue in your energetic body. That residue of hate and judgment stays with you, and ultimately blocks your blessings and creates a fog of negativity throughout your entire life; one that is recognizable to others!

Gossip is not just about speaking ill of someone else, it's also about allowing someone to gossip to you about someone or something else. The bottom line is this: if you can't or won't say it to a person's face, then you have no business saying it at all. Gossip is the lazy man's way of attempting to feel better about himself by bringing others down, and quite frankly, it's ugly. If you've got a reputation for gossip, we can almost bet that you've also got a reputation of distrust—because you've shown your true colors by talking about other people when they're not around.

Listen, in case you forgot, you're amazing. And you don't need to downplay or judge anyone else in order to make yourself look better. (You're already smoking hot in our eyes!) So if you do it, stop it—we promise it doesn't look good on you. And if you allow others to gossip in your presence (and think you're so innocent), know that you get to respect yourself by choosing to walk away. The only way to build integrity with our language is to PRAC-TICE it in the day-to-day, moment-to-moment instances that play out in our lives; and it may mean doing a complete 180 in the kind of people you associate with and how you've behaved in the past.

UPGRADING

In order to create a powerful life, we must be in the practice of upgrading our language. Let's be honest, most of us are completely lazy with our language and are unaware that we're digging a hole for ourselves in our conversations. We speak things into existence, literally birthing all that we fear most because of how we unconsciously speak about life:

"I could never . . ."

"I'm not smart enough . . ."

"No matter what happens, I always screw it up . . ."

"I have the worst dating luck . . ."

"They always cheat on me . . ."

"Money is evil . . ."

"There's never enough time . . ."

If most people realized the power that language holds to create and transform their lives, they'd be as determined to get their language in shape as they are about getting their bodies in shape. We have to be willing to catch ourselves when we use dirty words like "can't," "try," "have to," "always," "never," and "want" and upgrade to more powerful alternatives so that we can begin upgrading our lives.

DIRTY WORD or PHRASE	UPGRADE
I can't	I can / I choose not to
Try	Do or don't / will or won't
I have to	I get to / I'm blessed to
Always / Every time / Never	In this experience
I want	I choose / I welcome in

When you consciously choose to speak words of empowerment and possibility instead of words that are disempowering and finite, you create a potent environment for change. So watch what you say—the universe is always listening.

IS IT A FACT OR IS IT A STORY?

A part of radical responsibility with our language is determining whether we are dealing with facts or stories.

There are very few FACTS in the world; but you wouldn't know it based on how hard we are often fighting for what we label as "facts." Facts are simply what happened without any meaning, opinion, or judgment attached; the facts are just WHAT IS.

Now, the stories we create around the facts are a whole different matter. Stories are our interpretations of what happened: our opinions, beliefs, and judgments. All stories—and we do mean ALL—are made up and not true in the eyes of the world, even though they *feel* true for us. Stories, as lavish, amazing, painful, extraordinary, or ridiculous they may be, are simply our individual views of the world. Stories are where drama and upset live; facts are where they go to die.

Here are some examples of **FACTS** versus **STORIES**:

FACT: John arrived home at nine thirty in the evening after getting off work at five thirty.

STORY: John is late because he didn't want to come home and spend time with me.

FACT: Jess looked to the left while sitting at the outdoor café.

STORY: Jess checked out the cute guy who walked by the window outside the café.

FACT: I received a text message from Rob asking me how my day has been.

STORY: Rob is interested in me romantically.

So next time you feel yourself saying "the FACT is . . ." when you're fighting to be right, remember it's most likely not a fact, and more likely just your interpretation of what happened. Next time you find yourself building a story around what actually happened, stop yourself and get clear on what's real and what's simply your version of reality. When we can view the world through radical responsibility and with the understanding that most of what we experience has been created by the stories we wrote around the facts, we can walk with a lighter stride. The world doesn't seem so serious when we realize that we're the ones making it all up.

COMPLAINING

Complaining is really common in our culture today. We complain about what's not working with ourselves, our bodies, our health, our jobs, our friends, our partners, our government, and our world. We've become so great at complaining that it's now a normal thing to do in our conversations with one another, barely conscious that we're doing it in the first place. Sometimes we even end up in a complaining battle, each person trying to prove themselves or out complain the other!

"Today was the worst day ever; my boss totally blind-sided me with a new project."

"You think THAT'S bad—wait until you hear what happened to me!"

The very act of complaining means we have a reference point for something greater or more effective, but we're often not willing to do anything about it. We're focusing on what's *not* working and perpetuating that by sharing it with someone else, instead of focusing on a solution—how we could be making it work. You see, complaining is an easy way out. It's playing the victim and then using that to justify why our lives aren't working the way we wish they would. But if we take radical responsibility for our lives, we must be willing to look for the solution rather than at the problem; we must be willing to actually make a change to get the results we were complaining about not having.

Your complaint is your mission.

Use It Now

MAKE YOUR COMPLAINT YOUR MISSION

At first this may be tough to do, but it begins with bringing awareness to when you're complaining. When you find yourself going off about how something isn't the way you think it should be, pause and ask yourself, "Well, what do I plan to do about that?" This question alone has sparked a multitude of projects, videos, and ideas for both of us that have become wildly successful.

Preston's Story

I'm the cofounder of a social movement called The Love Mob, whose mission is to create organized acts of love all over the planet so we remember that love is what connects us. The Love Mob was formed because my friends and I got tired of complaining about all the separation, war, and lack of face-to-face connection that was happening in the world. I can remember sitting in a dusty tent in Black Rock City, Nevada, with Allison Kunath and Mustafa Shakir at a festival called Burning Man, having our very first conversations about it. We were complaining that nobody was coming together for love anymore in the major cities, and that someone needed to step up and do something about it. We noted that it was only at festivals or during major disasters that we as a species truly got to see people's humanity toward one another. And in a moment of true inspiration, we said, "Enough is enough." Within a month we created a Facebook group and set a date for our first Love Mob, and the rest is history. Because of our commitment to a solution, over five hundred thousand people have heard of or experienced a Love Mob. In essence, The Love Mob provides a place for community to grow, much like a parent provides for a child. We focus on self-development, creative expression, and acts of service and connection that affect our immediate and global communities. Out of a complaint came a mission and a movement that impacted hundreds of thousands of people around the world.

REMEMBER . . . YOU ASKED FOR IT!

So often we forget—especially when our problems seem overwhelming or insurmountable—that we asked for a bigger life. We asked for a life of incredible happiness, one full of purpose; for a crazy and amazing love like no other; for our dreams to manifest. We forget that in order to have a life this big, we have to have the capacity to hold it.

A lot of us want the "big win" but can barely stomach the small challenges. Many of us claim we're "ready for greatness" but refuse to take a look at ourselves first. The bottom line is, if you want to live an incredible life (and we're assuming you do, because you're reading this book, after all!), then you've got to be willing to stand in the fire. You have to be *the space* to hold the life you say you claim to want.

All of life is expanding you. The minute you make a big commitment, you better believe the universe is going to ensure you're ready to take it on. Often this means you'll be thrown all sorts of challenges to test your resolve, to determine if you're willing to release old judgments and patterns, and to ultimately face off with the deepest, darkest parts of yourself. If you're not, you'll just keep getting the same old results, because you'll be living with the same old patterns. It takes MASSIVE amounts of courage and tenacity to live an incredible life—to truly take yourself on and break your habitual patterns and beliefs.

We love to remind clients to use the stress of life to build strength. Here's a beautiful example of this in nature. When a butterfly first emerges from its cocoon, it goes through a tempering phase: it must strengthen its wings first by using them to break through the cocoon. If you opened the cocoon early, in an attempt to help the butterfly escape, it wouldn't have the strength to fly, because its wings haven't yet gone through the stress it needs to gain strength. EVERYTHING in life is an opportunity to create more resilience and a stronger emotional body to handle what you say you desire in life.

THE SHORT AND SWEET

You alone hold the key to your personal freedom, and that key is RADICAL RESPONSIBILITY. The moment you get that you're the author, the source, and the painter of your experience of life, you can shift into a state that you could've never imagined. This is possible through a radical acceptance of what is, uncovering the role you've played in what you're experiencing, building awareness around your language, and using your pain to propel you forward into your purpose.

THE HIGHLIGHT REEL

✦ When you choose radical responsibility, it means you had a hand in creating, allowing, or perpetuating everything about your experience in this life.

+ Life is impartial, always moving and always flowing. We suffer when we're attached to how life should be.

+ Responsibility starts with radical acceptance of people, circumstances, and situations as they are, not as we think they SHOULD be.

+ There is a difference between those who are victims to something outside of their control and those who continue to choose victim consciousness around an event.

+ Everyone and every situation are your teachers (especially those that annoy you most!).

+ A lot of us want the "big win" but can barely stomach the small challenges. Many of us claim we're "ready for greatness" but refuse to take a look at ourselves first.

+ Having integrity with our word is not just about having integrity with promises we make to others, but also about keeping the promises we make to ourselves.

+ There are very few FACTS in the world, and most of us live in the stories that we have created around the facts. These stories, while they may feel true for us, are simply our individual views of the world.

+ Your complaint is your mission. If you have a reference point for something better, do something about it.

POWERFUL QUESTIONS

1. Where do I notice myself still choosing victim consciousness?

2. Where am I out of integrity with who I say I am or with my word?

3. What is a complaint that I repeatedly have? What am I choosing to do about it?

STEP 3

Act Now

THE BRIDGE TO BREAKING THE CYCLE

You don't have to be great to start, but you
have to start to be great.
                    —Zig Ziglar

ow that we've built our awareness muscle and taken radical responsibility for our lives, what are we going to do about it? Sure, we can *know* all about personal development, have access to amazing distinctions, and have awareness of how we show up in the world, but if we don't *do anything* about it, it's just useless knowledge. We need to drop that knowledge into wisdom, and that happens when we put theory into practice. With our eyes wide open to the truth of what's been operating us, we can no longer sit back and wait passively for a miracle. We must act *now*. We must be willing to ditch the comfort zone of our automatic lives and get in the game! In this chapter, we'll touch on easy-to-use tools and distinctions that you can put into practice to start creating results *now*. We'll get into centering, blasting past your comfort zone, and becoming friends with fear; we'll take you through the freedom process and then talk about the gift of reframing our stories.

Yes, this will take work, but it will be oh so worth it when you look back on your life months from now and see where this journey has taken you. There is nothing quite as rewarding as a life well lived, the ultimate reward being who you become in the process; and you experience that by doing the work, facing off with yourself again and again, and *acting now.*

When we talk about acting now to override the system, it's important to note that having a positive and proactive approach to doing so is kinda the secret ingredient to this whole thing. We must change our perspective when it comes to what we call "the work" and celebrate when we find another opportunity for growth. Why? Well, most people get frustrated when they find yet *another* situation they need to "deal with." But in order to create sustainable change, we have to replace that frustration with celebration and joy, shifting our response from "Oh, NO, not another one!" to "Oh, YES! I found another one!" so that we actually look forward to finding these areas of growth, which ultimately transforms our relationship to change.

COMING BACK TO CENTER

> When you own your breath, nobody can
> steal your peace.
> —Unknown

We live in a world of constant DOING. We are always on the go, always in motion: work, running errands, responding to emails, engaging on social media, cleaning, cooking, buying, dating, playing, reading, etc. Doing is fantastic; it allows us to be productive and satisfies our urge to feel meaningful and filled with purpose. However, it's only half the story.

Our deep, unchanging core essence is not found in the DOING; it's found in the BEING—the still, calm place that is the basis of anything and everything we do. Some call it the soul, and some may call it the observer. We call this state of being our CENTER, and it's the place from which we have the space and clarity to make powerful choices.

When we get caught up in a constant state of DOING, we find ourselves on the merry-go-round of life. This constant state of motion creates a never-ending cycle of flux and doesn't allow any opportunity to do much more than react to what shows up. Imagine being on an actual merry-go-round (you know, the carousels with horses that float up and down and play really creepy music): because of the constant motion, you're really only able to engage with whatever is already on the ride. But if you saw something you wanted on the other side of the amusement park, you'd have to wait for the merry-go-round to stop moving (stop being in a constant state of DOING) before you could choose to get off and walk where you wanted to go. When we can tap into our center and access our inner stillness, we are able to bring awareness to all the doing, all the movement, all the options, and then make a conscious, calm, cool, and collected choice from that space of grounded awareness and perspective. It grants us a moment to pause, reflect, and feel into what is most aligned for our lives instead of reacting, or even responding, from a place of chaos or stress. If you're a smart little cookie and you consider yourself a champion multitasker, you may have graduated from pure reaction mode to response mode, but we've got a handy-dandy tool that's even *more* effective than your award-winning multitasking.

Full, deep breathing is the direct access point to your center, which sounds almost too simple—and yet so many of us rarely do it. Most humans these days feel completely overwhelmed and stressed-out by the daily activities of life, and we tirelessly search for a better way. That better way has always been right under our noses (literally!). Because it happens automatically, breathing is something most of us never have a second thought about. And if we want an all-access pass to a deeper level of self-trust and the capacity to handle stressful and overwhelming situations more effectively, consciously breathing from center is where it's at.

Have you ever noticed that during intense, stressful, or fear-filled times, the first thing to go is your breath? We tense and tighten up when our conditioned tendencies kick in, unconsciously reverting to shallow breathing. We tense the stomach, the jaw, and the shoulders without even really realizing it, yet we experience all sorts of stomach issues, back and neck pain, and the grinding of our teeth as a by-product. From an evolutionary standpoint, we automatically constrict our body in preparation for a fight. Back in prehistoric days, when our ancestors were worried about being attacked by saber-toothed tigers, they learned that by constricting their muscles when they were under attack, they had less of a chance of bleeding out and ultimately meeting an early demise. However, now that we're in the modern times of cushy desk jobs and iced vanilla lattes, that same fear response of constricting our bodies and our breath shows up when we experience modern-day "sabertooths"—breakups, inbox overload, public speaking, road rage, asking someone out on a date, or venturing into a new business deal—and the best way to override this stress response almost immediately is to bring awareness to our breathing and come back to center.

> Feelings come and go like clouds in a windy sky. Conscious breathing is my anchor.
> —Thich Nhat Hanh

Centering is an ancient technique that came from aikido, the Japanese martial art of spiritual harmony.

While we both had a general idea of the importance of breathing through our individual yoga, meditation, breathwork, and mindfulness practices, it was drilled home for us in a completely different way when we were students in a six-month training program with our mentor Scott Coady, the founder of the Institute for Embodied Wisdom. Scott's program had us in a rigorous practice of centering throughout the six months, and we routinely used it in the exercises and challenges he put us in. Through experiencing the results of using this tool, we saw how essential it would be if we were to continue building the lives we were committed to building. To call in a bigger life, we knew we would potentially be calling in more stress and overwhelm, so we knew that practicing this tool until it became second nature to us would be critical. We literally set reminder alarms in our phones for every few hours to "CENTER!" until it became an embodied practice. Now we center hundreds of times throughout the day, bringing our awareness to our inner stillness and wisdom.

Most of us nowadays walk around with our stomachs sucked in to appear thinner and our bodies tensed up with terrible posture and we wonder why we're so stressed-out all the time. It's because we're not fully breathing and allowing our bodies the space to relax and shake off tension and nervous energy. Centering is not just about taking some deep breaths and "calming" ourselves, it's about tapping into the physical energetic center of our bodies, breathing into it (make that tummy expand!), and transmuting ineffective energy. By taking it into our center to dispel it. It's about getting off the merry-go-round of DOING and coming back to our grounded core, where we have the time and space to make powerful choices instead of simply reacting to life. When our attention is on our physical center, it's diverted from the madness of the mind, and we can then move from a place of deeper wisdom, tapping into our intuition and intrinsic knowledge.

Centering is about taking all of our erratic nervous energy, then channeling and releasing it as we breathe through it. This simple yet brilliant tool will not only improve focus and expand what's possible for you (hello, choices!), but also reduces stress in high-pressure situations. Imagine what could shift for you if you took a few seconds to really tap into the wisdom of your body and create some mental space before a presentation, in the middle of an argument with your loved one, or in everyday chaos like email overload.

Use It Now

CENTERING

Okay, so you're probably wondering how this whole centering thing goes down. Here's the scoop:

1. *Stand in open-body position.* Stand with your feet shoulder-width apart, firmly planted flat on the ground (heels off, ladies!). Have a slight bend in your knees, so they're relaxed and loose, and draw your shoulders down and back.

2. Locate the physical center point of your body. Halfway between your navel and the top of your pelvis is your physical center of gravity. Place your hand on this area, between your navel and pelvis, as a guide.

3. Breathe into your center. Breathe into your center (think of bringing the inhale all the way down into the palm of your hand so it moves, rather than breathing into your lungs), feeling your stomach expand and contract as you breathe. Bring your attention to your breath, breathing slowly and deeply.

4. Release the energy. Release any tension in your body with each breath, scanning for constricted areas. If you feel extra tense in a particular area, tighten that area and then release it, doing that a few times until it loosens. Take all that energy and visualize it flowing down and out through your feet into the earth below, exiting the body on every exhale.

5. Practice. Now that you've got it down, it's time to practice. Practice, practice, and then practice some more until breathing into your center becomes second nature. Soon you'll be able to center without the use of your hand, or an extended, concentrated pause; you'll find yourself doing it mid conversation, while driving, sending emails, and even dancing!

We know, it sounds so *easy*. But it's often the small, easy things in life that are the hardest to do—and for us, this is definitely a game changer. Do not miss out on the opportunity to get off the merry-go-round and gain power, choice, and clarity as you've never known it before. The energetic space you create through centering will truly change the way you show up all over your life, and ultimately shifts the way the world perceives you.

OBLITERATING YOUR COMFORT ZONE

The comfort zone is where dreams go to die.

If you truly desire deep change and are calling in an amazing experience of life, you must recognize all the places where you're way too comfortable and begin the process of obliterating those areas one by one. Once you understand that fear is an illusion and the comfortable walls you've built to keep yourself safe keep out not only the scary stuff but also the extraordinary stuff, it then becomes your mission to continually burst out of the self-made prison you've been confined in. Quite frankly, most people aren't willing to stand in what we call the *testing ground* long enough to even begin to experience the pure possibilities that they asked for; most people avoid doing anything that makes them feel exposed or uncomfortable.

To illustrate going after your dreams, we love to use this metaphor in our workshops:

Imagine you're a sword-wielding warrior on a mission to storm the castle and save the maiden or claim your prince. But to get to the castle, first you must leave the comfort of everything you've known and set out into foreign territory. You soon enter the "Forest of the Unknown" (the TESTING GROUNDS!) and go to battle with the demons of the forest: mutant wolves, zombies, and fire-breathing dragons that are pretty darn scary. Once you make it past these intense forest dwellers, you come to the castle, but it's surrounded by a moat (dang it!). You notice the moat is filled with steroid-induced crocodiles that jump twenty feet in the air to block any sort of chance you have of crossing. But you just made it through the Forest of the Unknown past some crazy badass creatures, so you're feeling ready to take on these crocs! You fight your way through that final resistance and somehow, by sheer commitment and strength, you make your way across and FINALLY enter the castle to claim your prize! Sounds like a hell of a mission, right?

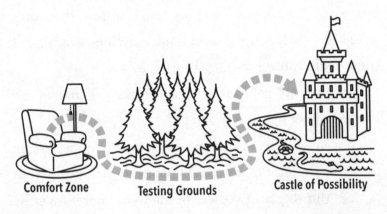

Comfort Zone   Testing Grounds   Castle of Possibility

You see, saving the prince or princess in the castle represents your dream or the intention you have for your life (pure possibility), but it's not always an easy journey to get there. The forest and all of its crazy creatures represent the testing grounds—the struggles, the roadblocks, and the setbacks that you must face and overcome in order to gain the strength needed to truly claim your dream. It's all the bumps and curve balls the universe will inevitably throw your way that are there to test your resolve and ultimately your commitment to achieving your dream. They're there to strengthen you, so you're ready and able for the next challenge that will inevitably come. The crocs represent the final test that is often the gatekeeper to our dream—that one final push that takes everything we've got to see just how dedicated we truly are. This is where most people quit.

The majority of people *start out* excited about a new possibility they've declared ("I'm going after this awesome castle!"), and it usually comes from a pain point or something they're fed up with:

"That's it! Enough is enough! I'm going to eat better and exercise and finally get my body back!"

"All my friends are getting married and having kids, it's my turn. I'm going to stop dating these guys who treat me like dirt and find my ONE."

And our all-time favorite: from around December 30 until January 15, everyone gets a gym membership, buys the book, does the course, and declares that "this is *the* year that things will be different!"

And then what happens? The minute they claim that they're going for the castle, they step into the "Forest of the Unknown" and the first wolf appears—they slay it and celebrate! WOO-HOO! But then the next one comes and the next one, followed by another and an-

ALEXI PANOS AND PRESTON SMILES

other, and slowly but surely they reach the point that they say, "Screw this! It's too hard!" and make their way back to the comfort zone, the safety net of what they've known, even if it's painful as hell. Meanwhile, what they didn't realize was each setback was actually a set up for their success; they were getting closer and closer to the castle. Sound familiar?

We've all been there time and time again, and it's unfortunate that some will go to their graves in their comfort zone after a few failed attempts to make it to the castle. And the catch-22 is the comfort zone that we think is supposed to keep us safe, secure, and protected from the unknown ultimately keeps us from the full experience of LIFE; in the comfort zone, we are cut off from possibility and are rarely able to access what we're truly capable of, leaving us feeling unfulfilled.

The moment you claim to be committed to something in your life, the universe, God, the infinite unknown (whatever name you have for it) will be sure to test that commitment so it can weed out the impostors. The moment you say you're committed to building out your business and becoming an entrepreneur, you'll get offered a hefty raise at your current job that you hate. The moment you say you're committed to your health and fitness, everywhere you go you'll be tested with candy, pizza, dough-nuts, and fast food (*mmmmm*, doughnuts). The moment you get clear on attracting the woman or man of your dreams, you'll be thrown a curveball of someone who's pretty great but clearly not the one.

The question then becomes, Are you willing to take the hits again and again and slay the dragons to move into the land of possibility where your dreams actually come true? Are you willing to be knocked down over and over again, but continue to get back up, because you know that on the other side of the testing grounds is the castle you've been dreaming about? The journey is not always going to be easy; you won't always slay every sin-gle dragon, and you may make it all the way to the castle and not be able to open the door. Understand that the results *will not* always be favorable, but *that's* where your commitment comes in.

We like to think of sports and how many shots are taken versus how many actually go in, or how after losing a game the greatest teams don't just throw in the towel because it didn't go their way. They get back in the gym and practice (win or lose!). They understand that when you commit to something it's a journey; and on that jour-ney the results won't always be in our favor—and quite frankly, that journey would be boring as hell if they always were!

Bottom line is, if you have unwavering commitment and resolve, eventually what used to be your ceiling will quickly become the floor from which you launch. Old standards of what's possible will be completely shattered and reframed as long as you're willing to push past the testing grounds. We know this because we're living proof of it. Neither one of us could've ever imagined being where we are now personally, professionally, and spiritually; but what we were clear on from the beginning was our mission in life, and no matter how many tests came, we *would* push through, NO MATTER WHAT.

Another big barrier to the land of possibilities and that big, epic dream life of yours is society's obsession with instant gratification; and we get that fix in the comfort zone where it's all warm, fuzzy, and familiar. We know what to expect and we begin to expect what we know. But there is absolutely nothing worse than knowing you wasted years of your life hiding out and not living up to your full potential—all for the sake of comfort.

Take being in a committed relationship, for example. Anyone can make a relationship work in the beginning, but can you be fully vested when all hell breaks loose?

Looking at the divorce rates all over the world and the number of messages we get about this subject, most people instantly bail when the going gets tough (testing ground!); they can't handle the blows when the dragons, wolves, and crocs come out. Instead, they end up blaming the person or circumstances for why it simply didn't work (that dragon is an ASSHOLE!), not taking into consideration where *they* weren't willing to go in their resolve or commitment to the relationship.

"He was too possessive."

"She was too insecure."

"We grew apart."

Whatever the complaint may be, we find that no matter where you go, there YOU are. You may leave the relationship, move to a new city, change your job or your wardrobe, but you will keep facing the same dragons and wolves over and over again, even if it's with a different person, until you're willing to face them from a place of radical responsibility.

FACING YOUR FEAR

The idea that you can be FEARLESS is a blatant lie. If you're human, you experience fears. From an evolutionary standpoint, fears are what have kept our species alive and kicking all these years. So it's not about completely obliterating fears altogether, putting on our "tough guy" pants and pretending we're a bunch of fearless robots; rather, it's about learning how to face our fears, understanding where they're coming from, and then deciding if they're worth overriding or not.

It's been said that at all times we're either living from FEAR or LOVE, and that everything else is an offshoot of these two powerful forces. We believe that the bravest among us, those we celebrate and the unsung heroes who we never hear about, are those who recognize the fear and choose to override it for the sake of their commitments. Ladies and gents, fear is here to stay. It is an absolute myth that anyone can be 100 percent fearless; however, what can and does happen is that we change our relationship with fear, becoming friends with it and converting it into excitement that can propel us forward.

In our teachings, we like to think of fear as a sign—a big flashing neon sign saying "CHECK THIS OUT!" Once we see the sign, we can look deeper into what it's trying to tell us. Often fear is trying to tell us one of two things: a major breakthrough is *right* around the corner and it feels scary because it's a total paradigm buster OR run like hell, this is no good for you. If you can decipher whether this fear you're feeling is because you're on the brink of magic or at the edge of disaster, you can navigate those feelings powerfully.

One example most of us have in common is learning how to walk. When we first tried to walk, the prospect of falling and getting scraped up was a real threat; but no matter how clumsy we were and no matter how many times we fell, once we truly understood that every stumble gave us insight on how to stand stronger the next time, we eventually learned how to walk gracefully (some more gracefully than others!) and never looked back. What once seemed super-scary and downright impossible is now something we don't even think about, all because we chose to face our fear and continue to override it until it passed.

Once we finally work up the courage to face our fears, what once seemed *impossible* turns into *I'm possi-*

ble; we realize it was never as bad as we'd imagined it to be. However, if we continue to be afraid of something, the fear often gets so big and so ridiculously out of control that we become completely paralyzed by it.

FAILURE? AIN'T NOBODY GOT TIME FOR THAT

Fear of failing sends many to their graves with their song still in them.

+ Setting out on an adventure of starting your own business . . . but not making any money.

+ Falling head over heels in love with an incredible person . . . only to have him or her leave you in a few months.

+ Setting out and losing weight . . . only to gain it back in a few weeks.

+ Taking yourself on and diving deep into personal development . . . only to feel you haven't made any progress.

Deep down, we ALL have a yearning for something, whether it be a new level of self-awareness or a new level in our careers; however, the fear of failing keeps us from taking the necessary risks and actions to make that dream a reality. Let's be honest, human beings HATE failure. It makes us feel all yucky inside, anxious, and downright embarrassed when it does happen. Most of us dip our feet into the testing grounds, get hit with one or two nasty failures, and instantly retreat back to our comfort zones—vowing to "never risk again." How absurd!! If you're reading this book, we know that you have a deep desire for pure awesomeness, and that comes with a certain level of risk to be and live that epic life. So we get to change our relationship to failure altogether and create a more powerful understanding of it.

Let's start with the basics:

Failure is just information. It simply presents an opportunity to grow. And just like failure, success is also an opportunity to grow. Both success and failure are neutral but hold within them immense possibility to sharpen your tools and get you back in the game, better than ever before. Both present us with the beautiful chance to ask ourselves, "What can I learn here?" Both success and failure give us some insight into what's working and what's not working and allow us to continuously better our best.

So instead of seeing failure as a setback, we can view it as a *setup* for success. It's a red flag that lets us know that there's probably a *more effective* way we could go about doing things. Yes, it sucks to not get the outcome we were expecting, but so what? Are we going to let one little setback keep us from living the life of our dreams? HECK NO! We're going to get up, dust ourselves off, and find another way to make it work (we're champions, remember?)! It's not just about achieving the dream or reaching the castle, it's about *who we become* in the process of getting there. Every failure is a growth point and an opportunity to expand who we are and ultimately what we're capable of. It's the journey that prepares us for the dream, and we simply can't just skip the preparation phase. And the cosmic joke is, once we reach that castle we'll have our sights set on a new one (because desire never stops), so we might as well enjoy all the moments on the journey, because THAT is what life is.

Use It Now

REFRAMING FAILURE

Here's our simple process for reframing failure in the moment, so we can get over feeling sorry about ourselves and move back into feeling awesome:

✦ *Remind yourself that it's just information.* When we're over feeling like crap about our "failure," we can stop qualifying it with *good/bad, right/wrong, better/worse* and see it for what it is: information. (But the key is, we have to actually get out of victim mode and stop feeling sorry for ourselves!)

✦ *What can I learn here?* Once we realize that it's just information (perhaps wrapped in shitty packaging), we can objectively ask ourselves how this can be an opportunity for growth. This is a golden nugget of a gift, but we have to accept the gift before we can unwrap it!

✦ *What am I committed to?* Remember when you said you were committed to that big vision of yours? Remember how juiced up you were about making changes and creating some new awesomeness in your life? Right. Don't forget that (especially now). Now is when we get to remind ourselves of how ridiculously committed we AC-TUALLY are to making this thing happen, double down, and keep pushing through the testing ground until we reach that damn castle!

✦ *How will I move forward more effectively?* Once we've unwrapped the gift, we can then decide how we want to use it as we reenter the testing ground, new and improved.

✦ *Prepare for lift-off!* Watch out, world, here we come! (And nothing can stop us!)

IT'S FREEDOM TIME

We can't break the cycles we've been living in until we understand that freedom is an inside job. In our work we meet so many people on the hunt for FREEDOM: financial freedom, time freedom, and the freedom to live life as they choose. But no matter how much money you make, how much spare time you create, or how many places you travel—if you're not free emotionally, you'll be a prisoner no matter where you're at in life or what's in your bank accounts. We've all met people with a ton of money, time, and resources to do whatever the hell they want—but they're not free. We also all know at least one person who doesn't have a ton of money, doesn't have a ton of spare time, and certainly isn't a traveling gypsy— but he or she is incredibly free.

Freedom is a state of mind.

While a lot of people in our world who are seeking freedom via external means (time, money, success, etc.) are truly on the hunt for internal, emotional freedom, most of us have never been taught HOW to free ourselves emotionally. So if freedom is truly an inside job, how do we tap into it? In our society, it's fairly customary to avoid our emotions at all costs because we take them as a sign of weakness; we tell ourselves to "get over it" or that we're "good."

But we are in-and-out beings: breath comes in, breath moves out; food goes in, food moves out; water goes in, water moves out. Emotions are no different: emotions come in, emotions must move out. Our emotions have to come out in order to complete themselves, but unfortunately we interrupt the full cycle of the emotion by stuffing it down, resisting it, and telling ourselves that we're "over it" when really we just packed all of that feeling deep into our subconscious mind, avoiding it at all costs. And after years of stuffing everything down, you better believe we have a junkyard of old, toxic emotions that we've been pretending aren't there.

Emotion is energy in motion—and when we stuff our emotions down and resist them (in the hopes that we're getting rid of those suckers), we are actually creating a ticking time bomb of stagnant energy. Our feelings keep stacking on top of one another and eventually they WILL come out, no matter the cost. That's why we're stressed out, angry, depressed, chronically fatigued, and always on edge. That's why we lash out at the person who cuts us off in traffic or at our children or loved ones. It's why we turn to food, drugs, alcohol, or sex to numb and distract ourselves from what's really going on. We can't keep throwing our emotions into the pressure cooker without expecting the lid to blow at some point and start spewing those emotions out all over our lives. Repressed feelings or emotions turn into anger issues, a short fuse, or an underlying feeling of hopelessness toward life. It's insidious. And it's not right or wrong . . . *but is it effective*??

Here's what it looks like. We experience something—let's say a breakup (a neutral event)—that we label bad (create a story/meaning), which generates resentment, pain, sadness, or anger (emotions). But before these feelings or emotions have an opportunity to complete themselves, most of us decide that we're "better off without him/her" and then make up a story about how we're relationally cursed and all men/women are assholes (stuffing down and resisting the feelings). All the while, we never allow the emotions to complete. Suddenly, we find ourselves angry at work or with our loved ones, quick to be triggered by small things that normally wouldn't aggravate us. This is because we have created an enormous amount of pressure from stuffing down our feelings, and those emotions must come out and complete themselves. It's like trying to force a beach ball under water; no matter how hard we try to press it down, the ball will keep popping up because its very nature is to stay afloat.

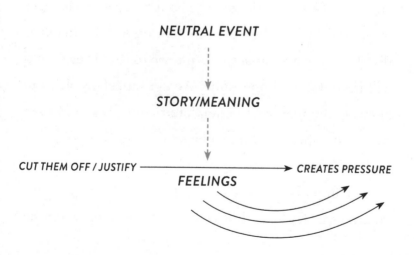

Children provide some of the greatest examples of how this tool works. They have absolutely NO trouble letting the feelings complete themselves in the moment, allowing them to pass through. One moment they're totally ticked off about Jimmy stealing their toy—crying, yelling, and allowing themselves to be ticked off—and the next moment they're back playing with Jimmy and the toy again. Truly, they got over it because they allowed the emotion to complete, allowing them to be friends with Jimmy, as if nothing happened. But after time (and tons of conditioning from adults to "shut up, toughen up, and stop *feeling* so much"), we begin to shut down our emotions, resist them, and stuff them down. We eventually become adults who will at one point be totally ticked off about being screwed over by Jimmy, and in the next moment convince ourselves that Jimmy is just an asshole and we're "SO over it, and will never talk to him again!" We cut ourselves off from allowing the feelings to complete themselves, and then we justify shutting them down to convince ourselves that we're okay.

It's important for us to get that we are *not* our emotions or feelings, but rather the observer watching them pass through. We are like the sky and our emotions are like the clouds drifting by; we are that unchanging, centered body of stillness that can objectively allow the feelings to float in and out without identifying *as* those emotions. Most people think of themselves as the *clouds* and forget that they are truly the wholeness of the unchanging sky. The more we call our feelings out and stop resisting them (hello, cloud!), the more they lose their charge and power, because in these moments we are identifying as the sky that is noticing the clouds passing through—and we begin to understand that the clouds are always temporary. Letting the emotions complete is about allowing what's coming up for you in the *present* moment around the event, not in your past concept of it; it's not about *what* you're allowing but rather *that* you are allowing the feelings and *being* with them.

If you look at the diagram below, you'll see what we call the Freedom Process (FP). Whenever we're feeling upset or emotional, we run through this FP to create some clarity around what actually happened and how we would like to move forward.

The Freedom Process (FP)

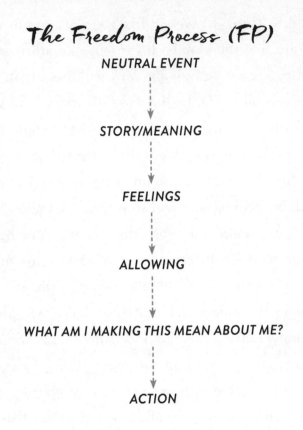

NEUTRAL EVENT

↓

STORY/MEANING

↓

FEELINGS

↓

ALLOWING

↓

WHAT AM I MAKING THIS MEAN ABOUT ME?

↓

ACTION

NEUTRAL EVENT: Our philosophy is that all events are neutral. They just ARE until we give them meaning.

STORY/MEANING: This is the meaning we assign to the neutral event, usually based on a mix of beliefs, conscious and unconscious agreements, our past, and our current mood.

FEELINGS: The story we assign to the neutral event will generate an emotional reaction, or feelings. This is where most people usually stop and cut off, justify, or stuff down the emotion.

ALLOWING: This is the process of surrendering to what you're noticing emotionally and physically without judgment, blame, or qualification; allowing WHAT IS to come through. It's about bringing awareness to and *being with* the feelings generated, allowing them to complete, while not identifying as them.

An example of how you would work the allowing portion of the freedom process is to think about an event that has a charge for you, and with your eyes closed or open, simply state what you're now allowing. This could be physical sensations, feelings, emotions, memories, or even things happening within the room that you're in. We like to remove any quantifiers like *"really* tight" or *"super* upset," as they are miniature stories about what *is*. When we are in the state of allowing, we need to stay away from story as much as we can, permitting the pure feelings to come through as they arise, moment to moment. We will call them out as if we're calling out the clouds that are passing through our sky, completely objectively. Don't judge what you're allowing; simply be present in the moment, creating a clear channel for whatever needs to make its way through to come through.

You can even pinpoint certain emotions or feelings that routinely come up for you and get to the source of them. We liken this process to seeing what's at the bottom of your emotion well. If we follow each link in the chain down the well, we'll eventually get to the bucket that's been holding one of the core, deep-rooted events or emotions that you need to complete.

For example, if Tom is doing the allowing exercise with the feeling of anger that routinely comes up for him, he would start with "anger" and just be with whatever next emotion or thought is triggered by that word. After he says "anger," he automatically links that to his father, which is linked to a memory of his being nine years old, playing with his dad's guitar and breaking one of the strings. His dad beat him with a belt, which is linked to shame and punishment. These two feelings link to him shutting down, which led to Tom bullying others in school and making them cry. Crying reminds him of his recent breakup, which is linked to distrust. Distrust gives way to

Tom's feeling of being abandoned by his father, which is at the root of his anger. Tom now has an arsenal of events linked to anger that he could go through the entire freedom process with. This is how we allow the feelings and events to complete themselves. Remember to *allow* the process to take you on a ride without judgment. This allowing leads you to an awareness of what may still hold an emotional charge for you, which is a major step toward emotional freedom.

WHAT AM I MAKING THIS MEAN ABOUT ME? Once you've allowed the emotions to complete themselves (let it out already, will you?!), then you can objectively ask, "What am I making this mean about me?" At this phase of the freedom process we create real freedom because we step fully into radical responsibility, release blame altogether, and choose to take ourselves on. Noticing what this event triggered within us that is still a pain point provides a massive opportunity for growth.

ACTION: Once we understand how we've assigned meaning to the neutral event and have allowed ourselves to be with the emotions and triggers that arose because of the meaning we assigned, we can then take action based on the question: What would be the most loving next step I could take that contributes to the highest good of this situation and all who are involved?

For example:

NEUTRAL EVENT: You're on a date, and a person sits at the table beside you and your date.

STORY: You create a story: You label this person as attractive, and your date eyed her the moment she came into view. "He's always looking at other beautiful women."

FEELINGS ARISE: "I am not enough. I'm ugly." You begin to compare yourself with her and feel emotions of jealousy and envy.

ALLOWING: Instead of lashing out at him or stuffing your feelings down and not saying anything, you could excuse yourself and objectively allow those feelings and the sensations they create in your body to come through, honoring them until they feel complete. You're recognizing you are *not* your feelings, rather, the observer watching them pass through. (As you become more attuned to this process of allowing, you'll find you can eventually do it in silence, in the moment, without anyone even noticing!)

WHAT AM I MAKING THIS MEAN ABOUT ME?

+ *Not enough:* I'm not enough for him and never will be. No matter how hard I try with my smarts, my looks, or my body, I'll never be enough for him or any man.

+ *Ugly:* I'm not attractive enough to keep a man's attention.

+ *Jealous:* I'm not secure enough to be okay when other beautiful women are around.

+ *Envious:* I wish I had what she had. I don't love and accept myself as I am.

+ *Comparison:* My hair isn't like hers. My eyes aren't like hers. My lips aren't like hers. My body isn't like hers. My vibe isn't like hers. She's better than me.

ACTION: Once we're clear about what we made this event mean, we can take action by making a *blame-free* request to our partner: "Hey, babe, I noticed that when that beautiful girl sat next to our table tonight, it triggered all sorts of emotions within me. I recognized that *I made it mean* that I'm not good enough, and I get that this is something that's *within ME that I get to work on*. I would love your support as I work through this; and my request is that you be patient and understanding as I do so."

When we're able to be with and honor what's coming up for us IN THE MOMENT instead of stuffing it down and ignoring it, we create REAL FREEDOM because our emotions no longer have us—we have them. You can use the freedom process in real time, as events occur with someone else, or even by yourself with past hurts and painful experiences. You'll be amazed at how much lighter you'll feel after you've created some physical and emotional clarity around the events that have shaped you in life.

TURNING PAIN INTO PERSPECTIVE

No one else can make you feel inferior
without your consent.
—Eleanor Roosevelt

As far back as we can trace, human beings have been sharing our collective history through story. Whether it was around a campfire or through ancient hieroglyphics, our lives consist of thousands of stories that can be told in many ways. Every time you open your mouth or put your fingers on a keypad, you're formulating a story about life as you see it. A story is something we tell ourselves and others to explain why we are the way we are. The question becomes, "How do we share our stories so they leave us empowered instead of feeling victimized, angry, or defensive?"

Preston's Story

I literally cheated my way through high school and college because of a story that I had no clue was running my life. This story had me isolating, controlling, and acting out in an attempt to feel worthy and good enough.

When I was around nine years old, I was removed from the "normal" class of about thirty or so children and taken to a class with the "slow learners"/mentally ill children. This was back in 1989, when they weren't quick to label kids as dyslexic. I will never forget the pungent smell of both stagnant mildew and bleach that filled the room, and the sight of building blocks made for toddlers on the table as they ushered me in as if I were a new prisoner. I had been tested a few times prior to being moved, but had never thought much of it. After all, I was a kid; the only things I cared about were recess, cartoons, and sports. But as they explained that this was going to be my new class, I felt a sinking feeling in my stomach and my nine-year-old mind started racing. "Am I dumb? Am I mentally ill? Oh no, I'm the dumb kid." This was a pivotal moment in my life because years later I found myself choosing cheating as the only way to get through academics—playing out and reliving that story of being "the dumb kid," letting it *have* me. However, when I decided to jump into a master's program in college, I made a new choice. I wanted to see what I was *actually* capable of and committed myself to completing my degree with absolutely *no* cheating. What I achieved in those three years was beyond what I ever considered possible for myself. With fierce commitment and tireless resolve, I graduated with a 4.0 and an enormous sense of pride in what I had achieved. It wasn't about the grades per *se, but about the integrity that I had chosen to demonstrate, and what living from that space brought me. It gave me the opportunity to write a new story about who I am and what I am capable of.*

Our stories, our wounds—the things that have happened to us and through us—are simply what they are. They are neutral events, no matter how brutal and unforgivable they may seem in our minds. We know, because we've worked with people who've experienced everything from sexual abuse as children to those who've lost their entire family to tragedy. We don't promise that this process will be easy or an overnight success, but when you rewrite your story and continue to speak about it from an empowered place, you will have the ability to shift what used to cause you immense pain and suffering into something that can evoke incredible strength, inspiration, and wisdom.

Okay, you ready to do this? Here we go.

Use It Now

REFRAMING YOUR STORY

Think about the biggest pain you've experienced, a secret you've been keeping in, or something that you've buried deep down inside. Really *be* with it. Use the freedom process from above to break down the neutral event, the story, and the feelings that emerge. Notice, be with, and allow them, then pick up with the prompts below:

+ What I've made this event from my past mean about me is . . .

+ How this story has held me back is . . .

+ If I continue living as a victim in this story, I will produce . . .

+ This happened *for* me because . . .

We can hear you now: "*For* me? What the hell . . . ?"

Yes, *for* you, because you get to look for ways that it was a gift. We've had people realize that without their drug abuse, they would've never found their deep spiritual connection; without their experience as a child refugee, they wouldn't have had the strength and tenacity to build a multimillion-dollar business; without their learning disability, they wouldn't have been able to develop the other senses and skills that are critical for their dream job. Look for how this event has brought you to a deeper, more effective understanding of yourself or of life. Look for ways that it's made you stronger, and how that strength has served your growth and expansion as a human being.

TURN YOUR MESS INTO YOUR MESSAGE

Turning your mess into your message is a powerful way to not only reframe your story but use it to make a difference in the world. One of the most powerful examples of this is the story of Mothers Against Drunk Driving, MADD. Candace Lightner started MADD after her thirteen-year-old daughter, Cari, was killed by a drunk driver in a hit-and-run on May 3, 1980. Now they have over three million members and supporters nationwide, and most important, Candice has created a movement that brings awareness to an important subject. There is no doubt that Candice would rather have her daughter back, but because she chose to reframe and own her story, turning her mess into her message, she has created something that has ultimately saved millions of lives.

Whether it was a nasty divorce, a heinous trauma, abuse of any kind, or something you may even deem minor like being bullied as a teen, when you reframe your stories and take your power back, your wounds turn into your wisdom—and you not only begin to fill your cup with newfound compassion and understanding, but all that goodness can then overflow to support others.

THE SHORT AND SWEET

Sustainable change comes when we are first able to create the space and stillness needed to make powerful choices from our center. We must be insanely committed to continue to step out of our comfort zones and play in the testing grounds, no matter what results we may get. When we can shift our relationship with failure and fear, we begin to welcome new challenges and opportunities for growth with enthusiasm and passion. In order to create *real* freedom, we must be willing to emotionally free ourselves from the stories and feelings that we've kept buried for years. Understanding that all events are neutral, we can rewrite our personal history and turn our mess into our message.

THE HIGHLIGHT REEL

✦ The first step to overriding the system is having a positive and proactive approach to doing so. We must change our perspective when it comes to what we call "the work" and celebrate when we find another opportunity for growth.

✦ When we can tap into our *center* and access our inner stillness, we are able to bring awareness to our daily activities, giving us access to clearer and more grounded choices.

✦ The moment you claim to be committed to something in your life, the universe, God, the infinite unknown, or whatever name you have for it will be sure to test that commitment. You must be willing and committed to make it through the testing grounds in order to reach your castle.

✦ Failure is just information. It simply presents an opportunity to grow.

✦ It's not about completely obliterating fears altogether, but about learning to face our fears and then deciding if they're worth overriding or not.

+ Freedom is a state of mind. If we're not free emotionally, we'll be a prisoner no matter where we're at in life or what's in our bank accounts.

+ Our emotions have to come out in order to complete themselves, but unfortunately we interrupt the full cycle of the emotion by stuffing it down or cutting it off, creating unnecessary pressure and stress.

+ All events are neutral. When we use the freedom process, we can notice the stories and meanings we've assigned to these events, allow the feelings to complete themselves, and then act from a place of love.

+ By reframing and rewriting the stories from your past, you can turn your mess into your message and use your insights to help serve others.

POWERFUL QUESTIONS

1. Where am I *not* willing to be in the testing grounds in life?

2. What event or emotion do I recognize that I may have stuffed down or justified? How has this held me back from a fuller experience of life?

3. How can you turn your mess into your message?

STEP 4

Own Who You Are

THE BRIDGE TO LIVING YOUR TRUTH

Seeking love keeps you from the awareness
that you already have it—that you are it.
—Byron Katie

Why is owning who you are such a critical step to having an epic life? Because if you culti-vate awareness, live from radical responsibility, and take action on your life, but you do it on *someone else's terms,* then there is no point. There is only one YOU, and that is your power. If you don't learn to own all of who you are and what matters to you, either you will create so much internal pressure that you eventually explode (hello, mid-life crisis!), or you'll just cut yourself completely off from the incredible *juice* of life and creative flow possible for all of us when we're aligned with our true selves. *Who you are* is already engraved on your soul; it's not a matter of needing to find it. It's about remembering, about peeling back the layers of programming we've been living behind and taking note of what's always been there.

In step 2, "Be Radically Responsible," we touched on how the context determines the content. Context is the *space*, while content is *what is contained in the space*. And a core principle of our teachings is that the CONTENT IS DETERMINDED BY THE CONTEXT.

For example:

CONTEXT: The sky

CONTENT: Clouds, sun, moon, stars, planes

***If we saw something that looked like a cloud in the middle of our living room, we wouldn't think of it as being a cloud like we see in the sky. We would potentially think of it as smoke or condensation.

CONTEXT: A drinking glass

CONTENT: Water

***If we saw water outside near land instead of in a drinking glass, we wouldn't consider it as drinking water; we would consider it a lake, pond, or ocean.

And if the context determines the content, then who you show up as determines WHAT shows up in your life.

CONTEXT: You

CONTENT: Relationships, Money, Health, Career, Family, Happiness.

We believe that when you OWN who you are, you become the space (the context) for the life that is truly meant for you (the content). By living and being the context of authenticity and realness, you become the space (a magnet) for authentic, harmonious interactions, occurrences, and content to show up. Owning all of who you are is such an important facet of extraordinary living, because we can then attract and create from a space of deep truth—and live a life that is truly aligned *for us*.

Many of the people we meet in our workshops and seminars are living on autopilot, not authentically. Therefore, the content they're getting is not in alignment with their higher selves, but rather a product of the masks they're living behind. They are so used to the status quo of society that they've completely lost touch with their souls, and autopilot has become their new normal. They end up having different identities or masks they wear when they're at home, at work, with their partners or kids, on social media, and with friends. They've gotten so used to living up to these false ideals of themselves they've forgotten the truth of who they actually are, and continue to attract people, circumstances, and things into their lives from that space of unconscious inauthenticity.

So what if you could unapologetically be the same person in *all* areas of your life? What if you could courageously shine that wild soul of yours out into the world and feel the freedom you've always been after? What would it look and *feel* like if you were fully in alignment with your truth? What could that attract?

OOOH! THAT gets us excited. Why? Because we know that when people step fully into the truth of who they are, the suffering on this planet takes a backseat to the joy, creativity, and communion that's possible when humans come into alignment with their truth. People around the world are desperate to be themselves, and YOU can be the one who gives them that permission, just by starting with owning all of who you are first.

If you're experiencing drama in your life, feeling stopped by all the shoulds you're trying to live up to, comparing yourself with others, or striving to get "somewhere," you may be experiencing what we call out-of-alignment-itis. This tragic illness of the spirit leads to terrible side effects such as a loss of enthusiasm, creativity, and joy in life . . . and it's completely unacceptable.

So strap in and get ready to uncover your driving force, blow up your box, kick your goals in the ass, and get naked all while owning the badass human that you are. Ready? Time to dive in.

THE FORCE WITHIN YOU

Coming into alignment with our true selves starts with knowing what DRIVES us. What do we actually care about? How do we spend our time? Where do we spend our money or give our attention? Knowing what forces drive our actions and behaviors is the secret sauce to inspired living. When we can first identify these forces, we can then align our actions with them. When this sync happens, it illuminates and inspires us, creating an untouchable force that permeates all areas of our lives and creates a sense of flow and fulfillment that we never could've imagined.

Take this ride with us . . .

Kate hated her life. But to the outsider, she lived a life most would dream of. She made a hefty six figures in a cushy finance job in New York City. She wore only the best and trendiest clothes on the market, always looking as if she walked off the runways. She dated some of the city's most eligible bachelors, and rubbed shoulders with the rich and famous. She was surrounded by friends and family who loved her, and even had time to volunteer during the holidays. She filled her free time with Broadway shows, amazing concerts, and the best sporting events of the year. She lived in one of the most desirable neighborhoods in the city, and had a summerhouse at the beach to escape to on the weekends. To everyone that knew her, Kate had the perfect life. And while she always had a smile on her face, deep inside she was dying.

At fourteen years old Kate loved the outdoors, painting masterpieces after school, and sewing together costumes that expressed her creativity. But once her parents announced their divorce, she made an unconscious decision that would change the course of her life. Kate's dad, who enjoyed the finer things in life and valued money, always looked down upon Kate's artistic interest, saying that the "artist's way will always leave you broke." Years later, when Kate's mom, who was also a bit of a free-spirited artist, filed for bankruptcy and lost the home she grew up in, that nailed home Kate's decision to "never be broke again." This led Kate down the path of becoming wildly "successful" in the finance field, chucking her artistic ways for a more "realistic" approach to living life, and ultimately pushing who she was aside, to live a life based on an *idea* of what she thought would bring her approval, control, and security.

Now, at thirty-seven years old, Kate is having a bit of a meltdown; recognizing that she doesn't even know who she is, and that she's been playing the game of being who everyone else wants her to be at the cost of not owning her true identity. She's been a chameleon of life—learning to adapt to the interests of her boyfriends and friends, doing whatever she could to maintain her financial and social status, and ultimately abandoning her own dreams, ideas, and desires so that she would never experience the pain of her childhood again.

Although Kate is an imaginary figure, she represents the culmination of the "ideal life" that the majority of the people we work with are after. We give this example because *most* people are yearning for a life that is completely out of alignment with what *actually* drives them most. And no matter how far up the social or financial ladder you may climb, if you're climbing someone else's ladder, you'll get to the top and realize it led you to someone else's ideal life, not yours. This is why we see so many rich and seemingly successful people numb themselves with shopping, food, drugs, or sex, and keep chasing the elusive "carrot" that never leads to satisfaction. It's why most of us are constantly looking to the outside world to help define us, because we have yet to go to work on defining ourselves.

Most people compromise, suppress, or just completely ignore what they're naturally driven toward in life, leaving them susceptible to LIFE defining them. The job, the money, the relationship, the religion, the friend, the parents, the nation—when we don't clearly define who we are and what drives us, it's as if the world decides on our behalf. And when that happens, people feel an overwhelming sense of being lost, misguided, and lacking in fulfillment.

So how does one liberate the most authentic and empowered version of themselves? Accessing their FORCE. Discovering and living from the core forces that drive you is the gatekeeper to a wildly inspired, fulfilling, and amazing life. And once you get clear on them, you can weave them into all of those areas that you have yet to experience success and fulfillment in. Defining what our driving forces are help define and shape our reality— they are the foundation with which we build our future on. And when we're moving from a place of clear definition, we then awaken our fullest potential. We access part of ourselves that feels superhuman—we can stay up later, wake up earlier, overcome incredible obstacles and challenges, and push through almost anything, if we're working from our driving forces.

Your driving forces are the specific things that truly move you, motivate you, and inspire you to do and be more than you are in certain areas of your life. It's the mother who can go above and beyond for her children, but not for her job. It's the child who can stay up all night playing video games, but falls asleep during class. It's the athlete that can push their body to the limit, but has never read a book. It's the things that we truly care about—the things that nourish and honor our innermost being; the things that make us feel FULL. Your driving forces are unique to YOU—yes, you and a friend or partner may share similar forces, but they will specifically manifest in a way that feels best for you. It's those things that you find yourself saying "I love to . . ." "I can't wait to . . ." "I get to . . ." and when you do those things you experience yourself in an effortless state of flow.

And as we mentioned earlier, if you don't clearly un- cover and define your own driving forces, you will let someone else's forces drive your entire life. You'll find yourself trying to live into and up to what society expects you to do; dictating how you should be spending your time and money, and leaving you feeling frustrated and unfulfilled in the process. When you're living by someone else's driving forces, you'll find yourself saying "I should . . ." "I have to . . ." "I'm supposed to . . ." and ultimately always feel a sense of resistance and struggle, essentially never getting the results you were after.

HOW TO TELL IF YOU'RE OUT OF ALIGNMENT WITH YOUR DRIVING FORCES:

+ You feel extremely busy, but as if you are getting nothing accomplished.

+ You feel an overwhelming sense of stress and anxiety.

+ You feel indecisive about what move to make next and conflicted about which path to follow.

+ You find that you compare yourself to others around you.

+ You're resentful of other people's success and place blame for why you're not where you "should" be.

HOW TO TELL IF YOU'RE IN ALIGNMENT WITH YOUR DRIVING FORCES:

+ You feel an overwhelming sense of purpose and fulfillment.

+ You experience the state of flow and ease, losing all sense of time and space.

+ You show up to challenges with a sense of confidence, patience, and determination.

+ You clearly move forward with direction, purpose, and conviction.

Use It Now

DISCOVERING YOUR DRIVING FORCES

Answer the following questions as honestly as you can possibly can. Don't write down what you *ideally* wish was the case, write what actually *is* the case—this is the only way to truly determine your driving forces.

1. What do I spend the majority of my extra money (money not used on basic living expenses) on?

2. What do I spend the bulk of my free time doing?

3. When I look at my stuff and the contents of my house, what does it mostly include?

4. When are you completely energized and motivated to show up fully?

5. What do you spend your time researching, studying, watching, or searching for online?

6. What are you always on time for, and what can people count on you for?

7. What lights you up, excites you, or can you talk for hours on end about?

8. When do you feel most "in the flow" or "in the zone"?

9. Think about a time in your life that you would deem one of your "best" moments or "peak experiences." What did you value most about that moment?

Now, look for the themes of these answers and write down the top three recurring ideas. For example, if you noticed that you spend your free money and time on rock climbing, biking, and other outdoor experiences—always talking about it and searching new adventures online, you would group those activities into a category that feels good to you like play, outdoor activities, or adventure. Each number below will represent one of three categories you'll choose.

1. _____

2. _____

3. _____

Ask yourself, "What does this mean to me?" For example, if one of your answers above is "play," you would ask yourself why play is important to experience flow, freedom, and vitality.

1. _____

_____

_____

2. _____

_____

_____

3. _____

_____

_____

By answering this question, you uncover your core or underlying driving forces. In this example play is the means to experiencing flow, vitality, or freedom. These are the core driving forces for that category.

Based on how often your answers appear and repeat above, create a list of your three most important driving forces and group them in order of priority, with your most important driving force first, and the least important driving force last.

1. _____

_____

2. _____

_____

3. _____

_____

Looking at your top three driving forces above, double-check that they are what you can *currently* see your life being guided by and not what you *aspire* to have your life guided by. This distinction is a crucial one, as we will use what drives you *now* to create momentum toward the life you aspire to create in the future.

The important thing to note here is it's about getting

honest with what really is driving you so you can use that force to bring yourself closer to the life of your dreams. When we clearly define what drives us and move to a space of alignment with that force, we mobilize all of our internal superpowers to do everything we can so that force can actualize. So, for example, while it may be more *idealistic* to say that your driving forces are love, contribution, and family, it's more effective to be honest about how what truly drives you is looking good (fashion), socializing, and winning.

Once you're clear that these top three driving forces are leading your current destiny, make sure you feel good about the order or importance. If you had to only live by one of these, would it be your number one choice? If it's not, whichever one you can't live without, make sure that's number one on your list!

YOUR INTERNAL COMPASS

It's important to understand that your driving forces are extremely powerful. They act as your internal compass to guide your entire life—moment by moment, choice by choice—ultimately creating your destiny. They point you directly towards to the situations that will satiate that driving force and will pull you away from those that don't. That's why love, money, health, and success feel so perpetually elusive to some, while others seem to be born with a golden ticket. It all comes down to what drives us.

So for any of you reading this that are experiencing a *void* in your life—you would like more money, the relationship of your dreams, to have a smoking hot bod, or to experience more joy in your life—the primary reason you don't have it yet is because you're not naturally driven towards those things. You may be into shopping instead of saving, craving attention instead of commitment, eating crap instead of eating healthy, focusing on gossip instead of focusing on gratitude. The bottom line is this: your life points to what your driving forces are; it's where you continue to spend your time, money, energy, and attention on (even if you keep *saying* you're driven by something else!). And all of your energy and attention will focus towards fulfilling those driving forces *at all times*—bringing you closer to those things that align with them and further away from those things that don't.

Let's look at the example of a man who earns mini-
mum wage, who would claim that his driving force is
financial independence. However, if you pull back and
take an objective view of his life, you can see he is
spending his money on eating out, drinking on the
weekends, wearing the best clothes, driving the nicest
car, and living in the best neighborhood. So is his driving force *really* financial independence? Or, is it more
than likely a driving force to look good and feel re-
spected?

Another example is the woman who says she want to
meet her "one" but says yes to any and every guy that
gives her a little attention, and eventually runs as soon as
the honeymoon phase is over. Is her driving force *really* a
committed relationship, or is it about attention and approval?

THE BIRTH OF A FORCE

In order to truly utilize the full power of your driving
forces, it's imperative to know where they came from in
the first place. We've found that most people's values stem
from a void—a perceived lack, usually attached to their
childhood. It's like being on a seesaw with an elephant on

the other end. The moment that elephant drops its weight on the seat, you go flying through the air. The moment someone has something they feel is lacking show up, it creates an opposite effect where the person looks to fulfill it to balance things out. The young boy who watches his mother and father struggle to put food on the table may have a driving force of financial independence, because out of that perceived lack he made a decision that he would never struggle financially. The little girl who's constantly compared to her proper older sister so often that she creates an identity as a rebel to stand out of that comparison. She then finds herself doing the opposite of what "good proper women" do. It's out of the perceived void that most people's driving forces are birthed.

You may be asking yourself, "Why is it important to know where it comes from?" Well, when you know what's feeding your driving force, you can decide if that void from your past is something you want to create from, or choose something else to create from. You can either choose to use the pain of your past to drive you to a new future, or you can choose to heal that part of your past and create a new driving force. There is no better or worse choice here, but you want to choose what *drives* you most, and own it with confidence.

Preston's Story

As I mentioned in a previous chapter, when I was in elementary school I showed early signs of a learning disability and was moved from the regular class to a special education class. Out of that void I developed a driving force of communicating with my voice and charming people so I would not be perceived as the dumb kid. I became a wiz kid at listening to adults, teachers, and television to expand my vocabulary. I wasn't great at reading and felt alienated by it, but I've used that pain to drive me to develop extraordinary speaking skills and discover alternative ways of learning that cultivated my genius.

Alexi's Story

One of the voids I experienced in childhood was the feeling that traditional education and religion never fully resonated with me. I felt a lack of challenge and inspiration, and that void led me down the path of seeking my own answers, and ultimately, my own truth. This void continues to drive me to this day, as I constantly feel like there is always a deeper cut to discover and never quite like to box myself into a traditional modality. I've also consciously chosen a more recent *drive of contribution. This came from a deep understanding and "a-ha moment," realizing that to me, fulfillment meant creating value for others and using my life and my gifts to give something rather than to get something. This new, more recent declared drive has become #2 on my list, second to growth.*

Use It Now

WHERE DO YOUR DRIVING FORCES COME FROM?

In the chart below, write your top three driving forces in the column on the left. Then, next to each driving force, go as far back as you can recall to see if you can identify when your driving force was birthed. Finally, decide whether you are choosing to fully embrace this driving force or if you want to choose something else.

DRIVING FORCE	WHERE IT CAME FROM	CHOOSE IT OR LOSE IT?

WHO'S TALKING?

We can't really own who we are if we aren't clear on who's doing most of the talking, first. We've found that at all times, one of two voices is doing the talking: the *higher self* (soul) or the *wounded self* (ego).

Tapping into the higher self or the wounded self is like changing the television to one of two channels, and whichever channel you tune in to determines what you experience. We believe that we are all born as our HIGHER SELF. We enter this world as whole, complete beings who aren't afraid to fully express who we are. And then somewhere along the journey, someone or something hurts us. We become wounded and begin to hide away parts of ourselves as a form of protection. Then we get hurt again. And again. And again. This creates a cycle that reinforces the false belief that we must hide our true, HIGHER self in the name of self-preservation.

These wounds can come from obvious sources, like verbal or physical abuse, or more subtle ones, such as always being told to keep your voice down because you are too loud. Whatever it was that hurt you, whether it was on purpose or not, has created a wounded self. And as

ALEXI PANOS AND PRESTON SMILES

we begin to operate from those wounds more frequently, we end up as adults operating from our hurt, thinking it's normal, never truly being able to uncover and therefore express our HIGHER self.

The wounded self is the inner voice that will have you believing that you're not worthy of anything. It constantly talks crap about you and everyone else. "You'll never get that job!" "You're fat, so he'll never even notice you." These annoying, relentless voices are the source of a lot of suffering in the world. The sad part is, most people have no clue that this voice of the wounded self is not actually who they are, but rather who they BECAME after they were hurt. The tricky thing about the wounded self is that it disguises itself as a helper. Its job is to protect you from more hurt by keeping you safe in the comfort zone, even if that's causing you immense pain. Do not trust that cunning little bastard, as it will have you stuck for a lifetime, slowly forgetting what your higher self feels like.

Now, on the other hand, when we rediscover our higher self, we are privy to a storehouse of goodies that all the great teachers of our time have tapped into. The higher self is where our genius lives. It's a direct line to source energy, opening life up to limitless creativity and harmony, not just with yourself but with all of life and its many creations. It knows that it can never be hurt, harmed, or endangered, and that it is the fullness of who you are. It's tapping into that limitless supply of love, brilliance, connection, and confidence. In a nutshell, the higher self is where it's at!!!

Use It Now

Here are five ways to tap into your higher self:

1. *Know that you are not your thoughts.* Thoughts are the content, while you are the context. Once you begin to believe in the higher self, you'll start to see when the wounded self is trying to sabotage everything to keep you safe, and you'll be able to stop identifying as it.

2. *Schedule in time for NOTHING.* Make time to do literally nothing but observe. Notice thought patterns, body sensations, and the gift of life, with no agenda other than to be still and witness. This may seem weird to you at first, but you must make space and time to allow your inner guidance and wisdom to speak to and through you.

3. *Commit to regular meditation.* We don't care if it's five minutes a day or thirty, when you add this practice to

your life, you reduce stress, improve concentration, and clear space in your brain for more positive thoughts.

4. *Dance Dance Revolution.* Dancing with reckless abandon is a surefire way to tap into the higher self. Once a week, find a place; whether it be a club, your car, or all alone in your room, to let yourself go. Dance like nobody's watching, and this will help you begin to recognize when you're in a flow state and when you're not.

5. *Mindfulness.* Being mindful simply means you bring an awareness to whatever it is you're doing at any given time. For instance, practicing mindfulness with one meal a day will bring an awareness that will be useful in cultivating a deeper relationship with the higher self. Challenge yourself to bring the utmost awareness to *one* task you do every day. We like to do this with our food, first taking a moment to honor its journey to get here, set intentions for it to nourish our cells, and then taking a fork- or spoonful of food into our mouths and savoring it, allowing the flavors to penetrate and invade our palates, chewing at least twenty times before going in for the next bite.

UNCLOG YOUR DRAIN

Owning who you truly are is about clearing the space for the fullness of you to show up. Think of this like a clogged sink. We've got years and years of gunk and debris that have entered our world; some of it flows right on through and keeps moving, and some of it ends up getting stuck, creating a blockage of flow. What sticks eventually creates a new reality—a new "normal" of what can flow in and out. The thing is, the universal tap of creative love energy is *always on*, but most of us are too clogged to ever fully experience it and let it permeate us. We get so used to the slow drain being our reality that we barely notice how the clog continues to get worse over time.

This drain is our channel, our access point to our true self and universal energy, and all of that debris is the negative people, circumstances, and things we take in mentally and physically; it is our beliefs, stories, fears, expectations. All of this gunk is in the way of experiencing flow with the fullness of our authentic self. It's hindering how much of the REAL us we can access.

So in order to really take on this process of owning who you are like a badass, you've got to first clear the drain and get rid of the gunk. You've got to pull out all those things that are getting in the way of your living an epic life so you can tap into the flow of the universe. When you begin clearing the space of past debris and become extra-conscious of not allowing any more in, you will begin to experience an unfolding of your inner truth and will have access to an insane amount of creativity, joy, and love in life.

So how do we do this?

BLOW UP YOUR BOX

An integral part of owning who and what we are is first understanding who and what we're not.

Doctor. Lawyer. Advantaged. Disadvantaged. Mom. Dad. Daughter. Son. Depressed. Shy. Old. Young. Black. White. Yellow. Brown. Easterner. Westerner. We assign ourselves thousands of titles and labels, but ultimately none of these are who we are; they're labels and parameters we've unconsciously assigned to ourselves that ultimately run our lives. We like to call all these labels, titles, and stories our *boxes*, because once you're in one, you're confined to the parameters of that space. In our work, we notice how people take the wholeness of who and what they are and tuck it neatly away into a perfect little box with one of many labels on it; a box that forever limits them.

So to put it bluntly, it's time to blow up your damn box. It's time to obliterate the constraints and walls that you've been confined to and limited by and build your own life by design, instead of living by default. And as fun as taking ten sticks of imaginary dynamite to your boxes sounds, it's not always so easy. Giving up the "lie" of who and what you've been living as to step into the full truth of who you are is no simple task. It takes wild courage, extreme bravery, and radical surrender. You must be willing to give up who you have been in service to who you're becoming or who you truly are. You must be willing to break free from the ball and chain that have been holding your true self back, but this also means stepping into the unknown. Instead of trying to live up to the beliefs, standards, and ideals that society has written for us, we must now have the tenacity to write our own rule book and live by our own standards.

Preston's Story

In the summer of 2011, I made a decision that my life was going to be dedicated to service. At the time I did what most would do and looked for "boxes" that I could fit in. Immediately, based on my skill set and because I was sharing videos on YouTube, I came up with the box of motivational speaker. I felt confident that I could take some courses and become one of the best in the business. I did a bunch of research and came up with a list of agencies I could reach out to and speaker boot camps I would attend, along with conferences that I could submit myself as a speaker for. I was so focused on becoming someone and something that my parents and society would be proud of that I began to lose *myself* in this process.

I attended seminar after seminar and kept getting the same feedback when asked what my topic of expertise would be.

"Love? That won't work. Nobody buys love. You need to be a peak performance or a leadership speaker. That's how you'll make it big."

In my heart of hearts this felt completely out of alignment for me, but I went along with it for a while and the result I was after seemed to elude me. Almost a year went by with what seemed like absolutely no progress. Until one day I got fed up and decided that if I was going to fail, I might as well do it on my terms.

So I hired a professional videographer and decided to share in my videos how I actually talk, not how I thought people would like to hear me. I began doing a thing that at the time I did not realize was channeling. I was allowing the messages to speak through me rather than trying to get it "right." Sure enough, within a week of releasing my first video with this new style of authentic sharing, I began receiving hundreds of messages from people all over the world saying that I was speaking directly to their hearts and they couldn't wait for more.

Instead of my signing with an agency and waiting for them to book me on speaking gigs, people, companies, colleges, and seminars began reaching out to me asking me to speak because they found and loved my videos. When I finally stopped looking for approval from the outside world and began to accept and embrace all of my wacky, passionate, loving, left-of-center qualities, I stopped having to look for work, because work came looking for me.

WHAT IS SUCCESS TO YOU?

When we take an honest look, we can often see that we've been living up to someone else's idea of what success is, and meanwhile never creating or choosing our own. But guess what? YOU'RE IN CHARGE. (That felt good to hear, didn't it?)

That's right, you're in charge of this whole operation. You get to decide what feels right for you and what a successful life would look like on *your terms*. Maybe success isn't about tons of money, a big house, a fancy car, and 2.5 kids. Maybe it's about having the ability to travel and not be tied down. Or perhaps it's about using your time on this planet to make an impact. Whatever it is for you—OWN IT. This is YOUR life, after all, so you get to decide how it plays out. You get to be bold enough to ask yourself some important questions. What would I try if I knew that I couldn't lose? What would feel absolutely amazing to wake up and do every morning? How do I want to spend my precious time on this planet? What is *my* definition of success?

As you begin to create and step into and own your unique version of success, be forewarned that some of your family members, friends, and cohorts may not agree with your choices. Often, when you go off and pave your own path, it can be extremely threatening to others, as their reality is completely dependent on the boxes that they've assigned themselves and you. But at the end of the day it's your life, not theirs, and living box-free is a bold statement that screams out "This is MY life, and I get to decide what's in store for me!"

Use It Now

So let's really define what success looks like on *your* terms. Time to bring back those top three driving forces of yours so that we can really create a new definition of success with them at the helm of your ship. First, you'll write your top three driving forces in order on the spaces provided below. Next, you'll write a statement of what it means to you to be successful with each driving force. For example, if "Freedom" is one of your driving forces, how will you know you've been successful in accomplishing the freedom that you're after? What does it look like for you? Perhaps success means "not having to answer to anyone but myself and my family, making my own schedule, and getting outside every single day."

1. DRIVING FORCE: _____

_____

_____

SUCCESS MEANS: _____

_____

_____

_____

2. DRIVING FORCE: _____

_____

_____

SUCCESS MEANS: _____

_____

_____

_____

3. DRIVING FORCE: _____

_____

_____

SUCCESS MEANS: _____

_____

_____

_____

Now, take all three of your success sentences and merge them into one overall success declaration that includes the essence of *your* definition of success. Consider this your success manifesto, your creed, your own personal mantra and mission statement. Rewrite this and keep this close to you, where you can see it everyday to remind yourself of what really matters *to you.* Use this declaration to align your actions, choices, and behaviors to your driving forces, and to measure yourself against it to see where you need to make some shifts and changes in your life, in order to move closer to success on *your* terms.

YOUR SUCCESS MANIFESTO

_____

_____

_____

_____

_____

_____

_____

_____

_____

_____

GOALS ARE BS!

While we're on this topic of designing success on *your* terms, let's talk about goals, shall we? Yes, we know that goals can be amazing and powerful and have you reaching all sorts of incredible milestones in life. But they're kinda bullshit. Yup, we said it. Yes, it's great to have things you want to work toward, but our human minds limit what is ACTUALLY possible for us because we live in a limitless universe. We cap our desires at a level that seems higher than where we currently are, but is essentially far too low based on what we are actually capable of experiencing. We ask for it, we receive it, and then it seems not to be good enough and we don't ever feel satisfied. Loads of books will tell you all about the importance of achievement through setting concrete goals, and goals do work if the goal is all you're after—but there's something more fulfilling that's available to us.

Working with thousands of people from around the globe, we hear people talk about all that they want to achieve: the money goal, the love goal, the stuff goal, the fitness goal, the career goal. But in actuality, it's never the goal they're after; it's the *feeling* that goal will give them. And more often than not, we're able to find those feelings in a million OTHER ways than just the single goal we've got our sights set on.

When we hold SO tight to one particular goal, our hands aren't open to grasp what may actually be better suited for us in the long run. A lot of times the universe sends us a version of what we desire, but we end up missing it because it didn't look how we expected it to look. For example, we ask for LOVE, expecting it to come from a relationship, all the while missing the unconditional love we're receiving from the new puppy we rescued. So we must set the intention on how we want to *feel* first so that we can then surrender to however that may end up revealing itself to us. When we go after the feeling, instead of the objective or specific outcome, this leaves room for miracles.

Alexi's Story

Setting goals kept me from my true self throughout my twenties. The problem with the goals I was setting was that they were based on a mix of what society expected from me and what my ego wanted me to do in order to feel validated. I was SO fixated on achieving my goals in television and modeling that I wasn't even paying attention to if they felt right for me. I just HAD to get to the finish line of the race I had started, no matter what. I climbed to the top of every ladder I had set up for myself (became a six-figure earner in the modeling industry and hosted several television shows on major networks), but I still felt completely empty at the end of the day. I had relied heavily on the notion that reaching those goals would bring me happiness, when in fact achieving them only highlighted that something still felt like it was missing. So I began asking myself how I wanted to feel, and this changed everything. I realized that underneath my goals was the need to feel worthy, secure, free, and as if my life mattered.

I began letting go of the idea of *how* that would show up and trusted that what I needed would reveal itself. Sure enough, my TRUE path began to unfold for me. I began following the feelings, and that created a whole new reality for me. Eventually I moved from New York City to L.A. because I wanted to feel more in touch with the mountains and ocean. I began a podcast because I wanted to feel as if I was sharing and making an impact, to meet amazing people and to be part of an inspiring community. That led to me creating inspirational videos because I wanted to feel like I was having an impact with my life and my skills, which brought me to where I am today. Transformational leader? Whoa, who would've ever thought? Certainly *not the girl from small-town Erie, Pennsylvania. I could've never guessed or worked toward the goal of doing what I do now, because this career path had never existed. It had never been done before the way I'm currently doing it.*

If you focus on the feeling you're after and make sure your actions, words, and ways of being reflect what you want to create in life, you'll have limitless opportunities to experience those feelings. Even more, when you attach your top three driving forces to your goals, you stir up all sorts of internal motivation and power to actually get it done! Which in turn leads to a more fulfilling life of gratitude, abundance, and real, lasting happiness that doesn't come and go with your changing circumstances. Owning who you are is about owning how you choose to FEEL, and making sure that your goals are aligned with your deep driving forces, so you *actually* move towards them! When you can get underneath what's really driving you, you can begin to create moments and experiences in life where those feelings can happen on a regular basis.

Let's look at a few examples of how to do this, with the case of three driving forces of adventure, growth and family:

GOAL: I want to clear six figures this year.

SO I CAN FEEL: Significant, secure, and free

WHICH I CAN ALSO FEEL BY: Reducing my cost of living, reducing my nonessential spending, and finding things that I enjoy doing that make me feel free.

HOW I CAN ATTACH MY DRIVING FORCES TO THIS GOAL: Every time I save my weekly amount, I will reward myself with time with my family, doing something outdoors where we're learning something new.

GOAL: I want to lose five pounds.

SO I CAN FEEL: Significant, secure in health, and worthy of love/recognition

WHICH I CAN ALSO FEEL BY: Committing to my highest growth and loving myself enough not to need the approval of others, focusing on loving my body with the best nutrition I can feed it, and moving it every single day. Work out because I love my body, not because I hate it.

HOW I CAN ATTACH MY DRIVING FORCES TO THIS GOAL: I'll choose workouts that get me outdoors. Every time I workout alone I'll listen to podcasts or audiobooks. I'll prep meals with my kids every Sunday and teach them about food in the process.

Got it? Your turn.

Use It Now

GOAL I WOULD LIKE TO ACHIEVE: _____

_____

_____

_____

SO I CAN FEEL: _____

_____

_____

WHICH I CAN ALSO FEEL BY: _____

_____

_____

_____

_____

HOW I CAN ATTACH MY DRIVING FORCES
TO THIS GOAL: _____

_____

_____

_____

_____

GOAL I WOULD LIKE TO ACHIEVE: _____

_____

_____

_____

SO I CAN FEEL: _____

_____

_____

WHICH I CAN ALSO FEEL BY: _____

_____

_____

_____

_____

HOW I CAN ATTACH MY DRIVING FORCES
TO THIS GOAL: _____

_____

_____

_____

_____

GOAL I WOULD LIKE TO ACHIEVE: _____

_____

_____

_____

SO I CAN FEEL: _____

_____

_____

WHICH I CAN ALSO FEEL BY: _____

_____

_____

_____

HOW I CAN ATTACH MY DRIVING FORCES
TO THIS GOAL: _____

_____

_____

_____

Now that you're clear about the *feeling* you're after and placed a little intrinsic motivation under those goals of yours, it's important to remember that we'll always be *after* something. We get to remember that we ARE nature, and *all* of nature is always *growing*. It's always moving towards life, and life equals growth. So while the top layer may be that we want more money—the car, the clothes, the status, the great relationship—the deeper cut is that we actually want to *feel* what we think those things will bring us. And the *deepest* cut of this whole thing? We are BORN TO GROW. With this deeper understanding that it really is all about who you grow into on the journey of getting to whatever goals it is that you're after, you can take a deep breath, let go of the attachment, enjoy the process, and stop taking yourself so damn seriously. It's ALL good, because it's ALL growth.

LET'S GET NAKED!!!!!!!!!!

We lead a workshop called "The Naked Truth," where we ask people to physically, spiritually, and emotionally strip down to their birthday suits and spill their guts about some of the most sensitive stuff they've been hiding from. And without fail, after EVERY workshop we do, we receive emails, texts, phone calls, and deeply connected emotional exchanges from people saying that they feel so free and light, and that life has not been the same since they began sharing their deepest secrets from a place of transparency.

Transparency? What the heck does that mean? Well, there's a *lot* of talk about vulnerability these days. They say it's the thing that connects us, the thing that makes us human. But the more we looked into vulnerability and worked with people all over the world on this topic, we realized that vulnerability still implies that there is something at stake or at risk, and one was operating from the notion that they could get hurt. Being *transparent* is about hiding nothing, simply being ourselves for the sake of being ourselves. It's about *owning* all of who we are, and caring *more* about honoring and respecting our true selves than caring about the opinion of others. Transparency says, "This is me, all of me, and I have nothing to hide. I'm not afraid to share myself because it's who I am, and I accept it."

We've found that the true entry point to owning who you are is really getting emotionally naked and transparent, which requires *radical* honesty. It's about taking off the mask and showing up as who we fully are, without being so attached to what "they" will think. The world opens up for us when we're willing to be honest with ourselves about how we feel, what we've been through, and what we're thinking. When we share our truth from a space of transparency, we create radical personal freedom, live from a place of pure possibility and create genuine and deep connections with others (and we get to be ourselves, which is pretty damn awesome!). Nobody, no matter how shiny their life looks on social media or television, is without issues. And when we drop the mask of perfection and allow others to see into our beautiful souls, we give them permission to do the same for themselves. But dropping the mask isn't always easy.

From a very early age we learn to wear masks to protect ourselves: strong, funny, beautiful, smart, athletic, stoic, the good girl / boy, protector, class clown / the performer, the bad boy / girl, etc. We play a role in order to fit into what we believe our parents, siblings, classmates, or society will reward us for. The problem with most of us is that we've been playing a role for so long that we no longer know or recognize who we actually are underneath it. This is why getting metaphorically naked is one of the keys to owning who we are. When we get into the practice of dropping the act and revealing our deepest fears and issues, they no longer have us, because there is nothing that we're running from or hiding from the world. We get to show up as *all* of who we are and are no longer at the mercy of validation from others.

Side note: This does not mean you go around emotionally dumping your stories on everyone and acting like a victim. It's about owning your stories from a place of radical responsibility (step 2, if you need a reminder!) and sharing what you're experiencing with those whom you trust.

At the root of most of human suffering is a lack of ACCEPTANCE—it's why we unconsciously wear masks in the first place. First, we don't accept ourselves, so we put on our mask and a show with hopes that others will accept that false version of who we are. When we gain praise and validation from that role, we become more reliant on the mask to feel good, becoming so attached to that validation that we get further and further away from the truth of who we are. Not only that, but disowning who we really are is a form of self-hatred; and this creates an endless and oh-so-familiar cycle of self-criticism and judgment.

Have you ever noticed how easy it is to criticize yourself—to point out all the ways in which you're not smart enough, pretty enough, small enough, big enough, etc? This negativity and pessimism is not only destroying your confidence but it's destroying your life. So what would happen if you actually treated yourself like someone you loved? What if you accepted all of you, just as you were?

We encourage you to take a hard look at this, because the moment you begin to accept who and what you are is the moment you're free. We firmly believe that there are no mistakes in the entire universe. Every single blade of grass, every baby born, every freckle on your face, and everything in between is here because it has a unique gift to express. We can't own who we are until we *accept all* of who we are. It can be easy to accept, own, and embrace the things that are deemed good in our society, but it's important that we accept, own, and embrace all the things that we usually run from; they are still a part of us, and what make us amazing. If we only embraced what's deemed acceptable in our lives, that would mean that we're embracing only half of who we are. In order to truly *OWN* our awesomeness, we need to own it *ALL*.

That means falling in love with your "dirty" past or shameful stories. It means embracing your curly, straight, kinky, or thin hair. This means accepting all your supposed failures and letdowns. It's about embracing your dark, light, and fair skin; about owning your crooked nose, high-pitched voice, razor-sharp elbows, linebacker shoulders, wild youth, sensitive heart, dry humor, monotone voice, and everything in between. It's time to start celebrating your uniqueness instead of trying to run from it. YOU. ARE. AWESOME. And it's time to own it!

KILL OFF COMPARISON

As we have mentioned before, there is only *one* you and THAT is your power.

You are a one-of-a-kind *masterpiece*. Out of all the billions of babies born on this planet, you have your own unique set of gifts, quirks, limbs, and language. You truly are remarkable and incomprehensibly unique. If we want to access our true power, we must be bold enough to access and own our *full* selves, without comparing that fullness to others. It's like being a beautiful flower with its own unique shape, pattern, smell, and size but then looking at all the other flowers and wanting to be like them. What a slap in the face to the brilliance that you are!!! What a total beatdown on the beauty that you bring! Worse, you're wasting precious time and energy checking out someone else's lot in life; time and energy that could be better spent shining all your goodness on the world.

It has been said time and time again that comparison is the thief of joy, and whoever said that has got a damn good point! When we compare ourselves to others, it's like a big flashy sign that reads: SCREW YOU, GIFTS! It's looking outside of ourselves at other people, circumstances, and things and feeling envious because we ultimately feel crappy about who we are and what we have.

The grass is greener where you water it.

A lot of us are peering over the fence of life, staring at our neighbor's yard and desiring what they have. We're watering their "grass" with our thoughts and desires; we're shining our light on it with our attention and time, and it gets greener and greener by the minute. You're coveting that job or the body of someone else; you want that life that's not yours. And while that's getting greener and greener from all your attention, the patch of grass you own is dying from neglect. This is how comparison works. It steals all your attention away from *your* gifts, *your* beauty, and *your* abundance and has you focused on what you *don't* have instead of what you do. And when your attention is on what's *out there*, everything seems so magical because you don't have to live in the day-to-day reality of what is; you just live in the fantasy of what *could* be. Your dying and depleted patch of grass was once the greener grass you admired from afar, but it's dying because YOU forgot to water it—and this is what happens when we are living in comparison.

So what if we watered our own grass and embraced ALL of who we are, knowing without a shadow of a doubt that not only are we enough, but we are freaking amazing? What if we put all our attention on our own space, on our own lives, and had gratitude for what we have and who we are? What if we killed off the beast named comparison and annihilated the thought that we are lacking in any way, shape, or form? What if we were able to admire ourselves just as much as we admire others? What we focus on expands, and what we appreciate *appreciates*—so if you want your life to thrive, you've got to get out of the comparison game.

Listen, it's not an easy thing to just *decide* to stop comparing ourselves to others—but we can decide to catch comparison when it rears its ugly head and knock it dead in its tracks. This will be a process at first, but the more you do it, the easier it gets. And soon enough you'll notice that you'll stop feeling so envious and begin to appreciate all the beauty, wealth, and abundance around you because you can appreciate it *within you* first.

There is only ONE you—and that's what you're here to be. Stop trying to be everyone else, because life will always feel like a struggle when you're trying to live up to and into someone else's world.

Use It Now

KILL OFF COMPARISON

When you notice yourself comparing, stop and follow these three steps:

1. *Call out comparison.* By calling it out, you are training your subconscious mind to bring awareness to it every time it happens. When you notice yourself looking at others with an envious eye, call it out internally. "I see you, comparison, and you're not going to win this time!" Building this muscle will make life easier for you as you dive into the process of victoriously overriding the beast!

2. *Acknowledge what you're comparing.* Whether it's someone's hot bod, amazing partner, cushy job, or flashy stuff, acknowledge how amazing it is, and better yet, share that acknowledgment with the other person!

Then bring attention to whatever it is about this that triggers lack within you and show some gratitude for what you *do* have.

For example, let's say you're comparing someone's beautiful looks to your own. You would first acknowledge how much of a hottie the other person is: "Damn, she's beautiful! / You are STUNNING!" and then get honest and recognize where that comparison came from— maybe because you thought you weren't as beautiful as she was. Then it's time to get grateful and acknowledge your own beauty, your own hotness—how you are KILL-ING it right now, too!

3. *Humanize it.* Often when we are in a state of comparing we are idolizing other people and not seeing the whole situation for what it likely is. Yes, they may be beautiful, but we don't know what they're dealing with emotionally. Yes, they may have more money than we do, but we don't know the struggle they may be going through with their family. When we can take a step back and humanize the person or circumstance, we can see that there is always more than meets the eye.

YOU CAN'T FAIL

*You cannot go anywhere to get what you
already have, and you cannot do anything
to become what you already are.*
—Hale Dwoskin

YOU. CANNOT. FAIL.

Let that marinate in your consciousness for a moment. If we could be with you in the flesh, we would do the happy dance with you. This is a monumental truth, so please let this penetrate your cells. No matter how bad it may get, no matter what you may be up against, you cannot fail as long as you are living, as long as you have breath. So many people are engulfed in trying to "make something" of their lives that they miss the life they have and who they already are. Approval, control, and security are what most people are seeking in the world, and as long as those are at the helm of the ship, those people will always be off course from their true selves. And let us be clear, there is no right or wrong way to do life, but when life is done on your own terms, it's a hell of a lot more enjoyable.

The thing to get is *there is nothing to get*. There is nowhere but *here*. There is nothing that will make you better or more deserving because you already are and have everything you need. It's not about becoming, it's about *revealing*. When we can drop this idea that we need more, have to be better, or need to be different, then we can start truly owning all of what we already are and shining our unique light out onto the world.

As simple as it sounds, the purpose of life is to *live* it . . . and to be ALL of ourselves while we do. The purpose of all of nature is to thrive so we can ultimately be and share the wholeness of exactly what we are. Once we understand this concept, we can then get that owning the gift of who we are is truly the *only* thing that matters. From this space of pure possibility, we can ask ourselves: what do we choose to create NOW, and *why* are we choosing to create it?

THE SHORT AND SWEET

There is only one YOU, and that is your power. No matter how bad it may get, no matter what you may be up against, you cannot fail as long as you are living, as long as you have breath. Success is what you define it to be, and only you can live your truth and own who and what you are. YOU'RE IN CHARGE. There is nowhere to go and nothing to get. It's all here now. When you blow up your box and rework what you're going after with an understanding of what you desire to feel and understand what truly drives you, you move from "trying" to the *living embodiment* of the life you've always imagined.

THE HIGHLIGHT REEL

+ If you don't learn to own all of who you are and what matters to you, either you will create so much internal pressure that you eventually explode (hello, midlife crisis!) or you'll just cut yourself completely off from the incredible *juice* of life that is possible for all of us when we're aligned with our true selves.

+ At all times one of two voices is doing the talking: the *higher self* (soul) or the *wounded self* (ego).

+ The higher self is where our genius lives. It's a direct line to the source, opening your life up to limitless creativity, harmony, and pure, unadulterated abundance.

+ When you begin clearing the space of past debris and become extra conscious of not allowing any more in, you'll begin to experience an unfolding of your inner truth and will have access to an insane amount of flow in life.

✦ It's time to obliterate the constraints and walls you've been confined to and limited by and build your own life *by design,* instead of living by default.

✦ It's never the goal we're after; it's the *feeling* that goal will give us. And more often than not, we're able to find those feelings in a million OTHER ways than just the single goal that we've got our sights set on.

✦ We've found that the entry point to owning who you are is getting emotionally naked and transparent, which requires radical honesty. The world opens up for you when you're willing to be honest with yourself about how you feel, what you've been through, and what you're thinking.

✦ It's not an easy thing to just *decide* to stop comparing ourselves to others—but we can decide to catch comparison when it rears its ugly head and knock it dead in its tracks.

POWERFUL QUESTIONS

1. If I was truly brave and knew I couldn't fail and wouldn't be judged, what would I do? Who would I be?

2. How do I actually want to *feel* in life?

3. Without all the labels I have attached to myself and the boxes I have put myself in, who am I?

STEP 5

Have a Blast

THE BRIDGE TO VITALITY

We don't stop playing because we grow old; we grow old because we stop playing.
—George Bernard Shaw

There's a ton of beautiful personal development work out there that supports humanity in having an incredible life, but a lot of it is missing a critical element: FUN! A common misconception in the personal development space is that the work has to be serious, highly emotional, and deeply intense. But if we're not living it up and enjoying our moments on this planet, we're missing out on the best part of the human experience.

So don't be so damn serious! When's the last time you laughed until you thought you would pee your pants? When's the last time you danced the night away or allowed yourself to not have it all together? This is what so many are missing. We've gotten so caught up in chasing the carrot that we've forgotten to enjoy the journey along the way. We firmly believe that the F word is where it's at. In fact, we schedule it into our lives, making sure that we never forget that none of this matters if we aren't enjoying ourselves.

We believe that having a blast is truly the missing ingredient, and that no matter how much you "know," how deep you've gone into this work, how many certifications or degrees you may have, or how many retreats you may have participated in—if you're missing the element of fun, you're missing the whole damn thing.

Remember, life is just life. It's going to bring us highs and lows, ups and downs, tsunamis and sunny days; and it's all here for us to decide what to do with it. Do we complain about it and ho-hum our way through the day? Or do we dance with life and make the most of it? We've all met those people who have such an incredibly cheerful disposition, no matter what's happening. Those are the people we love to be around because they lighten the load for all of us. We've also met people who are always taking things far too seriously and way too personally— and those are the people we tend to avoid like the plague.

Bottom line: LIGHTEN UP. You only have one chance at this lifetime in this particular skin suit, so why not make the most of it? Why not squeeze all the juice that you can out of all the lemons that life throws at you, and do it with a smile on your face the whole time. Remember, you've got LIFE . . . how sweet is *that*?

So if you're ready to dive in and get your fun on, keep reading for some tools on how not to just follow your bliss, but BE it.

LIFE IS WHAT YOU MAKE IT, AND HOW YOU SHOW UP TO IT

CARPE DIEM! Yes, yes, we see this phrase all the time in online memes and on T-shirts and motivational posters, but how many of us are actually seizing the day? Are you taking the proverbial bull by the horns and enjoying what life has to offer? Or are you simply in reaction to life, playing out the same old boring routine day after day? Life is what *you* make it, and you'll always get a direct reflection of how you show up to it. Cranky all the time? Life probably doesn't look so good to you. Beaming rays of sunshine from your smile? Life is probably pretty damn good. The minute you decide that life is shit, it is. Conversely, the minute you decide life is awesome, BOOM! The train to Awesome Town shows up.

Life by its very nature is not "easy," but we do have a choice in how we show up to it. Some pray for rain and then complain about the mud. It's all a matter of perspective and choice.

One of our favorite sayings is "This too shall pass"; it points to the flow of life, how everything is always circulating. The issue comes when we stop flowing with life and start swimming upstream. We fight life, trying to make it something other than what it is. We suffer because we're expecting it to work out the way *we think it should* rather than being okay with what actually *is*. And when we can show up to what *is*, rather than showing up to life with our expectations of what we hope it will be, we can choose to make it mean anything we want. We can choose a different perspective: find the joy in the mundane, the beauty in the breakdown, and the magic in the mess. What a powerful thing to know that no matter how "bad" it may seem or how caught up you've been in the struggle, in a single moment you can stop, center, and choose *joy* now.

We have a friend named Steve (one of the most intelligent, loving, charming Frank Sinatra aficionados on the planet) who embodies this beautifully. He can tell you anything about Sinatra, the Rat Pack, and anyone associated with Frank Sinatra at the time. He can hold his own with you about what's going on in politics or what's been shifting in the world lately. He'll school you on some history you've probably never learned about in school, and he'll tell you what books to read if you want to dive deeper into that topic. The best part is, he's a peaceful man who is full of so much joy and really *gets* what it means to connect with another human being. Oh yeah, Steve also happens to live on the streets of Los Angeles, with his shopping cart and his stack of books, including one very large anthology on Frank Sinatra, which we bought him as a gift.

Steve has shared with us on many occasions that the average human being is missing the mark for buying into the "rat race" without actually enjoying any of the things we work hard to accumulate. And he's got a solid point! Collectively, we spend our time working forty to sometimes eighty hours a week, busting our behinds and going to the point of exhaustion—for what? So we can have nice things we never get to enjoy because we're exhausted on the weekends from working so damn much? Steve says that he's living what true freedom is and that life is beautiful for him. At the ripe old age of sixty-three, Steve wakes up at about five thirty every morning, drinks some water, does some push-ups, cleans himself up, and goes on his morning walk, in which he collects cans to recycle. By one in the afternoon, Steve is settled under a beautiful tree in Pan Pacific Park (where we first met him), hanging out reading and philosophizing with whoever will join him for a chat. Steve is having a blast and is doing it on his own terms. He's free and choosing to make his life work *for him*.

We share this story about Steve because he truly personifies this powerful lesson. Steve gets that life is always life-ing and that he has a choice in how he will live it. He chooses to live on the streets and push a flower-draped cart because that's what makes him happy. So whether you choose to live like Steve or choose some fancier digs, make sure you're choosing to have a blast while you're doing it. Because at the end of the day, what good are all your accomplishments, degrees, houses, and cars if you're not actually enjoying any of them?

BREAK UP WITH MONOTONY

Monotony sucks. And it kills joy like a dose of cyanide will kill life. No matter how excited you are about that new item of clothing, that new phone, new job, new house, or new person, you'll eventually become accustomed to it, and the novelty (and dopamine hit) will wear off. No matter how much we love certainty and the security of the known, we as humans have a deep yearning for change. We like to call this the shiny new toy syndrome, but technically it's called habituation. Shiny new toy syndrome is where you get so used to something you once loved and couldn't get enough of because it became such a normal and consistent part of your life that you are no longer psychologically or emotionally stimulated by it. Therefore, you look to new people, places, or things to offer a sense of newness and a shot of feel-good dopamine to the nervous system (shiny new toy!).

A lot of people think that this will never happen to them, and when it does, they feel depressed or sad because the novelty eventually faded away. Then they set their sights on something new, thinking THAT will be the answer to their happiness problems, only to repeat this never-ending cycle. So how do we beat this and have a blast in the process? Well, first we must adjust to it and know that it's inevitable. Yes, you will begin habituating to that new career, that new level of success, and that new person who seems oh-so-amazing right now; but you beat shiny new toy syndrome by mixing it up and breaking up with monotony.

This is a two-part process:

1. Decide that you are the bringer of your own have-a-blast-ness wherever you go. It's not in the cars, in the money, in the significant other or hot date; rather it lies in your ability to say "Bring on the blast!" *You* are the party starter wherever you go, whether you're by yourself or with a hundred other people.

2. Switch it up! Do something different. Challenge SAME and go for UNORDINARY. Take a different route to work. Dress differently. Try a new restaurant or explore a new group of friends. Take a class in something you've never learned before. Spice things up with your partner and do the unexpected. If you want to create that rush of NEW to the brain and body, YOU'VE GOT TO CREATE IT.

So stop complaining about being bored and start getting creative, dammit! Mix it up, and challenge yourself to stretch and explore parts of yourself you never knew existed!

Use It Now

Today, mix it up by finding three strangers to engage with. Whether it's in the elevator, at the coffee shop, or in line at the grocery store, chat it up with someone you would normally avoid.

WHAT TURNS YOU ON?

Joseph Campbell famously whispered, "Follow your bliss," and the world took note. The problem with following your bliss is you end up being the annoying tagalong of bliss, instead of the creator of it. So we took this statement and sprinkled some epic dust on it, turning it into *BE YOUR BLISS*. That's right, we want you to be so deeply connected to what turns you on that not only do you live it, but *it lives you*. It can't help but come out of your pores and overflow onto everyone you meet, because it has become an integral part of who you are.

In order to truly be our bliss, we must come into deep communion with what turns us on. You know, those things that make you feel so full of joy and excitement that you lose all track of time, laugh until your stomach hurts, and can't help but take a deep sigh at just how amazing life is? YES. THOSE THINGS. That's what you get to spend more time doing. And if you read that statement and wondered to yourself if you can even remember the last time you felt those feelings, it's GAME TIME.

It's time to stop focusing on trying to survive, to make a name for yourself, to get it right, and to get through another day. It's time to stop being so caught up in work and struggle, and start doing more of what turns you on and makes your heart happy. Make this a priority and you instantly up the amount of aliveness you feel on a day-to-day basis.

STORY TIME:

One day Jack, a wealthy businessman from the big city, took a trip to Mexico to get away from the stress of his day-to-day operations and enjoy some solid rest and relaxation. The minute he touched down, he went for a stroll on the beach, where a fisherman caught his eye. With a huge smile on his face, this man was unloading the day's catch from his ragged little boat. Jack thought to himself that fishing would be a great way to unwind, so he approached the man and paid him cash to take him out on his boat the next morning. The next day Jack and the fisherman headed out to sea, and because the man knew the water so well, Jack caught many fish.

Jack was so impressed with the skill of the fisherman that he used his brilliant business mind to devise a plan: "You're so talented at this that we could easily get you tied into some of the best restaurants in the city, which would make you more money. More money could eventually get you a better boat—heck, a whole fleet of boats—which would bring in loads of money as you scale up your business! You have no idea how much money you could make!"

The fisherman replied, "Well, that sounds lovely, but what on earth would I do with all that money?"

Taken aback, Jack said, "You could invest it. Buy some property, build bigger businesses—you know, the usual!"

With a straight face, the fisherman asked, "And why would I want to do that?"

"Well, so you could eventually retire and do whatever the hell you wanted to do, I guess. THAT'S what money can buy you. Freedom! What would you do if you had that kind of freedom?"

"Well, sir," the fisherman said with a smile, "I would take my little boat out and go fishing."

The moral of this story is that if you are living your bliss, being and doing what turns you on, you'll never have to take vacations from your life or count on retirement as the time you can finally enjoy life. Enjoying life now is *the* secret of people who are truly free and full of joy.

So what turns you on?

Use It Now

★ As a kid, what did you *love* to do—something that you could do for hours on end?

★ Think of the last time you can recall when time totally stopped and you felt immensely content afterward. What were you doing?

★ What is your favorite way to spend your free time? What lights up your soul?

Whatever you listed above, start scheduling more of that into your days. Make it a priority. Do what turns you on, and do it often.

FOCUS OUT

Want to be floating on rainbows and dancing in the moonlight because you're so filled with joy? Create value in the world.

Research shows that excessive focus on material gains and the acquisition of more success and stature actually leads to a *decrease* in happiness. We spend so much time focused on *getting more* for ourselves that it creates a kind of self-obsessed loop of not-enoughness. On the contrary, focusing out—*giving more* and creating value for others—is actually the secret sauce to attaining happiness and un-shakable confidence. Yes, creating value for others may not sound as glamorous as climbing to the top of the suc-cess ladder, but it can generate within you an abundance of awesomesauce that you can pour all over yourself and on the world.

Doing good and creating value for others doesn't just have a wondrous side effect of happiness, it actually *causes* happiness. In our workshops, we have a challenge that we send our groups on in which they have to create the maximum amount of impact in the world during one of their ninety-minute breaks. When assigned this stretch, the groups feel a bit overwhelmed and frustrated at first, focusing on how they're going to generate the *maximum amount* of impact. Once they come to an agreement on how they're going to do this, they head out to see what they can create.

What was first a challenge to see how much they could get (external gain) almost always turns into how deeply they can give. They realize about fifteen minutes into the exercise that the point is not to "get" as many people as they can, but rather to create depth and meaning with the people they do encounter. Without fail, when the groups return from this challenge they enter the room dancing, singing, hugging, and laughing, with the biggest smiles on their faces and sparkles in their eyes. Did they receive any physical gains during this stretch—more money, status, respect, or stuff? No. They GAVE. They gave only what they had in their hearts and in their souls, and they were left with a feeling of unbridled joy.

As simple as it sounds, when we see that we are capable of creating and generating value for others, we then see ourselves as a person of value. It's like a shot of caffeine to our soul and our self-esteem. When we create value for others by focusing out, we come to know ourselves as a person filled with value that can be shared with and appreciated by others. Knowing that we have that value to give lets us know that we are, in essence, *valuable*. And when we consider ourselves valuable, we move through the world with confidence, clarity, and happiness.

Use It Now

BE A SECRET SERVICE AGENT

Find a way to secretly give or perform a random act of kindness. It could be something as simple as leaving a random love note on someone's windshield, sending flowers to someone at work, or mowing your neighbor's overgrown yard. Whatever you choose to do, do it secretly so you can enjoy the feeling of giving without the expectation of a return.

THE SHORT AND SWEET

Life and personal development don't always have to be so serious. When we can tap into the juice of life, we can tap into the joy of it. By shifting your mind-set, switching things up, doing what turns you on, and focusing out, you have the ingredients for a concoction of bliss and joy that will add a little more pep to your step. Remember, if you're not having fun, you're not tapping into the magic that life has to offer. So get your blast on!

THE HIGHLIGHT REEL

✦ If we're not living it up and enjoying our moments on this planet, we're missing out on the best part of the human experience.

✦ Life is what *you* make it, and you'll always get a direct reflection of how you show up to it.

✦ When we can show up to what *is*, rather than showing up to life with our expectations of what we hope it will be, we can choose to make it mean anything we want.

✦ No matter how excited you are about that new item of clothing, that new phone, new job, new house, or new person, you'll eventually get used to it/him/her and the novelty will wear off; so switch it up! Break up the monotony and create some newness in what seems mundane and normal.

✦ BE YOUR BLISS. Be so deeply connected to what turns you on that not only do you live it, but it lives you.

✦ Doing good and pursuing altruistic outcomes doesn't just have the wondrous side effect of happiness; it actually *causes* happiness and generates confidence.

POWERFUL QUESTIONS

1. What things did I love to do as a child?

2. How can I bring more fun, wonder, and spontaneity to my life?

3. What legacy do I want to leave behind? How will I use my gifts to serve and create joy for both myself and others?

NOW WHAT?

One of our biggest pet peeves is meeting peo-ple who have all the knowledge about *how* to live an incredible life but don't *use* it. They can spit off the best of the best from the literature of psychol-ogy, personal development, and spirituality; they've read the CliffsNotes versions of the bestsellers on all the book lists. But when you look at their life and the results gen-erated by it, you're underwhelmed. DO NOT LET THIS BE YOU!

Yes, there is a lot of great information in this book. But if you don't actually use it now, it's just information. Information becomes *wisdom* when we put it into prac-tice, using it again and again until it eventually becomes second nature to us. Will you get it right every single time? Certainly not. But you'll have the awareness and know-how to access the tools because you've developed a deep relationship with them by being in the *habit* of using them.

Know that you're going to have moments in life that challenge the crap out of you. Know that you are going to want to say "Screw it!" and quit. Know that the minute you make a declaration for a "bigger" life, you will get tested on that declaration (testing grounds!). Remember, if you want to experience an amazing life, you have to be able to handle *and hold* it. And in order to be the space for that new kick-ass life of yours, you're going to have to keep showing up to the challenges with your game face on and your commitment steady.

Giving up and settling back into your old routine is *easy*—too easy! So you've really got to challenge yourself to stay in the work and be in the dance, and keep reminding yourself of the five steps.

Any time you feel faced with a challenging situation, reflect on these five steps and then adjust as necessary:

1. What do I need to be *aware* of here?

2. How can I take *radical responsibility* for this?

3. What *actions* do I need to take *now*?

4. Am I *owning who I am* or acting from my wounded self?

5. If I'm not *having a blast,* what do I need to shift?

With these five steps you truly do have a road map to an epic life. Now it's up to *you* to USE IT. Let this be the day that changes everything for you, the day you look back on and remember the commitment you made to being extraordinary. Let this book be the reminder for you that you have everything you need *right now* and it's just a matter of whether or not you choose to activate it.

It's NOW or it's never. The choice is yours.

ACKNOWLEDGMENTS

We acknowledge the divinity within you.

If you want more inspirational goodness for your journey, be sure to check out our website:

WWW.ALEXIANDPRESTON.COM

Or you can dive deeper with our 12-Week Online Training Intensive:

THE BRIDGE METHOD
WWW.THEBRIDGEMETHOD.ORG

An uplifting read with stories to inspire confidence and action steps to actually change your life.

"Alexi is the next generation of thought leader, paving a path with her incredibly unique and down-to-earth approach."
—JACK CANFIELD, COAUTHOR OF THE BESTSELLING CHICKEN SOUP FOR THE SOUL® SERIES

PICK UP OR DOWNLOAD
YOUR COPY TODAY!